BURGESS AND MACLEAN

Burgess and Maclean

by ANTHONY PURDY and
DOUGLAS SUTHERLAND

LONDON

Secker & Warburg

Contents

ACKNOWLEDGEMENTS   7

1. ELEVEN YEARS AFTER   9

2. THE OFFICIAL VERSION   18

3. THE GREAT DEBATE   34

4. BURGESS, THE BACKGROUND   45

5. THE MACLEANS   92

6. DAY OF DEPARTURE   121

7. AND NOW, MELINDA   132

8. PAPERCHASE   144

9. SECURITY?   165

10. AT HOME IN EXILE   180

POSTSCRIPT   190

5

Acknowledgements

THE AUTHORS wish to acknowledge with more than the usual thanks the very large number of people who have contributed to this book. Many must remain anonymous for a wide variety of reasons, but others include Arthur Christiansen, Frank Owen, Tom Driberg, M.P., Lt-Col. Marcus Lipton M.P., Stephen Harper (*Daily Express, Moscow*), John Miller (Reuter's, Moscow), Percy Hoskins (*Daily Express*), Donald Seaman (*Daily Express*), Morley Richards, Ross Richards, and Norbert Trautmansdorff.

We have quoted from the following books:

Guy Burgess, Portrait with a background, by Tom Driberg (Wiedenfeld and Nicholson).

The Missing Macleans, by Geoffrey Hoare (Cassells).

The Great Spy Scandal, edited by John Mather and Donald Seaman (*Daily Express*).

Herbert Morrison, an Autobiography (Odhams).

I

Eleven Years After

A BLACK POLICE car edged past the parked lorries of Covent Garden and swung into Bow Street police station yard. Two men stepped out briskly and, unnoticed by anyone, walked through a side door.

Inside, a large crowd of reporters waited. Some chatted to the duty sergeant; others sat on the oak benches scrutinising the day's list of offenders, or stood staring out of the windows. There were more journalists than usual that day. Two wealthy company directors were appearing on a charge of living on immoral earnings, and the newspapers wanted every word of what was said. It was a slack period in Fleet Street, and news editors had to make the most of anything that was offered. If anyone had, therefore, wanted to find a large number of crime and court reporters that morning for any reason, then Bow Street would have been the first call.

In the spacious, book-lined office of Sir Robert Blundell, Chief Metropolitan magistrate, the two men from the police car were being handed by him a signed warrant for the arrest of Burgess and Maclean. The clerks and secretaries who quickly knew about the warrant were astonished. Had the missing diplomats come back, then, where were they? They knew that they would soon be reading the answers.

9

Det-Supt. George Gordon Smith of the Special Branch, and Mr. Peter Palmes of the office of the Director of Public Prosecutions, shook hands with Sir Robert and left, the warrant now in Smith's briefcase. But instead of leaving by the side door, as they had arrived, the two men strolled into the main hall of the court building. Their appearance brought every reporter to life. The presence of these two, together, could only mean the beginning of something big.

"What's going on, George?" "Anything for us?" "Who are you picking up?" The questions came quickly as the journalists sensed that Smith was in a friendly mood. In one sentence, and with a twinkle in his eye, he told them what had happened. There were gasps and whistles of astonishment, then a dozen men dashed for the telephones outside.

The *Evening Standard*'s next edition was only ten minutes away from deadline; the *Evening News* had twenty minutes to go. Both managed to squeeze the story on to the front page. By the time the presses were rolling, newspaper offices throughout Britain were moving into top gear. All had the same messages over the teleprinters from the Press Association and Exchange Telegraph: "Warrants out for Burgess and Maclean. They are expected back from Moscow tonight or tomorrow."

At 2.25 p.m., Scotland Yard's Press Bureau issued this statement: "There are grounds for supposing that Donald Maclean and Guy Burgess may be contemplating leaving—or may have left—the USSR for some other territory. In order that they may be arrested should they come within the jurisdiction of our courts, warrants have been applied for and issued for their arrest for offences under Section One of the Official Secrets Act, 1911."

Section One of the Act deals with the gathering of information in prohibited places, the making of plans, sketches and models etc., or the communication of any secret official code word or password which is "calculated to be, or might be, or is intended to be, directly or indirectly, useful to an enemy". The maximum penalty is fourteen years.

Within five minutes of the Scotland Yard statement, teleprinters in Reuter's Moscow Bureau in the Sadova Samotochnyaya chattered out the news. Robert Elphick, head of the bureau, grabbed a telephone and dialled the number of Burgess's flat overlooking the famous Novaderchy Monastery. The call was answered by Burgess's friend, the curly-haired ex-miner, Tolya. He said that Burgess was away on holiday and would not be back for three weeks. Efforts to telephone Donald Maclean failed; he had changed his telephone number.

But John Miller, also of Reuter's, knew where Maclean lived. He drove to an eleven-storey block of apartments beside the Moskva river, took a lift to the sixth floor and rang the bell of the brown-painted door. A crew-cut youth with black horn-rimmed spectacles, wearing a bright red shirt, answered. It was 18-years-old Fergus Maclean. Miller asked in Russian: "Is Mr. Frazer at home?"

Fergus answered in English: "I will see."

Maclean then came to the door. He snapped: "I've got nothing, absolutely nothing, to say to you."

Miller asked: "Do you know about the warrant?"

Maclean looked over his shoulder to where his son and 10-years-old daughter Melinda were standing in the hall. Then he said: "I've asked you not to come here. I have nothing to say. I've nothing against you personally, but I just don't want to speak about anything to anyone. Please go away. Goodbye."

Two hours later Mr. William Hatch, area manager in Amsterdam for British European Airways, telephoned his London headquarters from Schipol with the news that Burgess and Maclean would be flying into London from Amsterdam on BEA flight 439, timed for touchdown at 10.10 p.m. This message was passed on to reporters at 6 p.m.

Fleet Street newsrooms immediately ordered teams of reporters out to Amsterdam, to catch flight 439 and fly back with the two fugitives. Blanket coverage was ordered for London Airport; high-powered cars and motor-cycles were lined up ready for the race into London after the arrest of Burgess and Maclean at the airport. Some went to Gatwick, in case there was a diversion of the flight. Extra men went to Scotland Yard.

On the first floor of Television House, Kingsway, Geoffrey Cox, editor-in-chief of Independent Television News, was sitting behind his huge desk holding a conference about the night's news bulletin, already replanned completely after the report of the warrants at midday. Then, at 6.15, he was handed a slip of paper telling him of the expected arrival at Amsterdam. He read it out; the meeting was electrified. Crisply, he alerted department heads by phone, and in between calls issued a stream of instructions to mould one of the biggest news-coverage operations in ITN's history.

A huge team of outside broadcast men were sent to London Airport—cameramen, lighting and sound technicians, interviewers and reporters. A camera crew was flown to Amsterdam. Four simultaneous telephone calls were put in to Moscow—to Reuter's office, to ITN's Moscow correspondent, to the British Embassy and to Burgess's flat. Within twenty minutes, about one hundred people from Television House alone were working on the story. Then began the task of finding screen time. But the problem looked insoluble; clearly, the normal news programmes could not accommodate the material that might flow in, yet advertising time and scheduled programmes are so rigidly patterned as to be inviolable. Or were they? Geoffrey Cox spent half an hour on the telephone, with the result that, for the first time, all the ITV companies gave permission for their programmes to be interrupted at any moment during the evening for live broadcasts from Amsterdam or London Airport. These live "inserts" were to be as long as necessary; in other words, the ITV companies gave *carte blanche* to the news men for the whole evening. It could have been one of the most expensive nights in television history.

In Amsterdam crowds of reporters, photographers,

newsreel and TV men spilled out on to the Schipol runway when KLM flight 302 arrived from Moscow. That was the plane on which Burgess and Maclean were supposed to be travelling, before changing to the BEA flight. Arc lamps lit up the silver and blue airliner and armed Dutch police lined the aircraft steps. Out stepped sixteen passengers, bemused and bewildered by the lights and the crowds. None of them looked like Burgess or Maclean.

One man was suspected and questioned repeatedly, but he maintained: "I am John Edwards. Who is this man Burgess, anyway?" Eleven people were escorted to a coach and driven to BEA flight 439 bound for London.

In London, an impatient throng of Press, radio and television men were waiting for the 10.10 touch-down when the news reached them that neither Burgess nor Maclean were on the plane. No one believed it. Reporters continued to chain-smoke in the corridors and conference rooms; photographers checked and re-checked their equipment. Then came a rumour that the flight had been diverted to Herne airport. That was checked, and it was found that there had been a fifteen-minute delay at Amsterdam, but that the destination was still London. Still, some newspapers sent off more men, to Herne, just in case. . . .

At 10.30 the BEA plane landed and slowly taxied to its parking position in front of the long sightseers galleries. In each oval window, clearly visible under the airport tarmac floodlights, was a pale face. The passengers could already see the batteries of cameras lined up at the edge of the apron and wondered who among them was the object of this extraordinary attention. As the turbines slowed to a whisper, airport police surrounded the aircraft, and two black cars drew up at the foot of the gangway. It looked as if the message from Amsterdam had been another bluff, that the diplomats were on the plane after all.

The television arc lights focused their hard bluish brilliance on the door as the steps were locked. It opened, framing a stewardess. Then came the passengers. One man stepped out, his head and shoulders covered with an overcoat. He hurried down, to be stopped at the bottom by the waiting police. The cameramen surged towards the group, taking pictures as fast as they could.

Was it Burgess or Maclean?

The man suddenly shrugged off his overcoat and laughed at the photographers. Then they too saw the joke. He was a *Daily Mirror* reporter who had caught the plane at Amsterdam and decided to pull the leg of both his colleagues and the police.

While all this was happening in Amsterdam and London, Reuter's John Miller drove again to Maclean's flat. This time, the door was opened by a middle-aged, bespectacled woman with a slight Cockney accent, believed to be the daughter of the late Harold Laski. Miller handed her a Reuter's message from London which said: "A BEA spokesman said tonight in London that Burgess and Maclean are flying from Moscow on a plane scheduled to arrive at Amsterdam."

Maclean appeared in the doorway as she was reading

15

it. He looked very angry, and shouted: "Shut the door! Shut the door!" The door was slammed in Miller's face.

So Maclean was known to be still in Moscow, anyway. But where was Burgess? His flat mate, Tolya, said after Easter that Burgess had telephoned him from Yalta and told him to tell callers that he had gone abroad and would not be back for at least three weeks. Then he began to worry about the effect of the mystery he was creating. He flew back to Moscow to clear up his position by issuing a short Press statement that he was still in Moscow and that he intended to stay there.

He phoned this to Reuter's from the 27th floor of the Ukraine hotel, from the room where Jeremy Wolfenden, the Old Etonian friend and correspondent of the *Daily Telegraph*, lived. That statement caused some of the fastest car driving that the Russian capital had seen for some time. Stephen Harper of the *Daily Express* tore across the city in his Ford Zodiac to see if Burgess was at his flat. Walter Lister of the *New York Herald Tribune*, who had been lunching with Harper, trailed him there. Tolya answered the door and said that Burgess was at the Ukraine hotel.

The two reporters then raced to the hotel and took the lift to the 27th. It stopped first at the 20th, and John Mossman of the *Daily Mail* stepped in. He had gone direct to the hotel but had mistaken the floor number. All three newsmen burst into Wolfenden's room together—much to the consternation of their colleague and their quarry.

Burgess was lying on the bed, his Old Etonian tie

16

loosened and his shoes off. He sat up, took a gulp of
Canadian Club whisky and said: "I'm not saying any
more than I have said in the statement." Wolfenden was
putting typewritten sheets into the drawer of his desk.
For half an hour, then, Burgess parried the questions
expertly—"I wasn't a Foreign Office spokesman for
nothing, you know." Finally they left him, to file their
"interview". . . .

2

The Official Version

FORTNUM AND MASON. Nervo and Knox. Burgess and Maclean. In eleven years, two Foreign Office diplomats have become a national institution by their absence. In the words of *The Observer*, "they are the only current British thriller to have been running longer than *The Mousetrap*".

Their names are linked inseparably, like those of a big store or a stage partnership. But they created something more than either; an historical enigma, seemingly insoluble. When they vanished, they took with them much more than a boxful of atomic secrets, military plans or chemical formulae. They equipped the Soviet leaders with first-hand knowledge, a unique report, on The System which governs Britain and, to a large extent, the West. They could explain motives and policies; they could name names and reveal the strengths and weaknesses behind those names; they could pass new judgment on the past and give fresh forecasts for the future. In Moscow their value, perhaps, was transitory. Perhaps it was not. There is no way of knowing. In Britain the interest has endured. Not solely because of the legend sustained by the Press. Burgess and Maclean may not be important in themselves. Nor are they symbolic, for of what can they be symbols? But they do

represent the crumbling of the Image of the Establishment in Britain, the image of a corporate body of men,
all Caesar's wives, whose little foibles and eccentricities
could be looked upon indulgently and even encouraged.
(Scientists were something else altogether—Nunn May,
Fuchs, Pontecorvo; too clever by half, and probably
foreigners, anyway.)

The defection of Burgess and Maclean, however, in
whom so much trust and confidence had been placed,
was a savage, shattering blow, not only to the Establishment, but to national pride as well. If this was possible,
what next? Who else? No one could even guess, and
eleven years later the guesswork becomes more difficult.
As case histories, however, Burgess and Maclean remain
unique; they are a reflection on the system that produced
and maintained them. They are a warning and yet, in
some odd ways, a cause for thanksgiving. For in revealing
our weaknesses to others, they revealed our weaknesses
to ourselves—which may not be a bad thing, after all.

There can be no pretence that this is a full and accurate
account of what happened to Burgess and Maclean, from
their university days to the present moment; there are
too many conflicting accounts, too many "reliable" and
contradictory witnesses, too few indisputable facts. But
one fact that *is* indisputable, that emerges from all the
work and the research and the interviews, is that the
story is by no means ended. Many mysteries remain;
mysteries that, while unsolved, serve to protect important reputations. It is here that a rather sordid story
becomes sinister.

Many people know the names of the "guilty men"; as one newspaper called them. Many people know the names of the persons who told Burgess and Maclean that it would be wise to flee; they know who, and how, and when. In a criminal case, they would be accessories, but here, the plea of "national security" has been used to fog the issue and smother enquiry.

In the past few months, however, since the farce of the "arrest" warrants, interesting answers have been given to specific questions, and these throw a new light on the whole story. They reveal the real status of the two men in the Foreign Office; their extraordinary friendships; how they were warned and by whom, and how they managed to vanish without trace. But these facts pose yet another question: who are the men in Britain powerful enough to manipulate events of national importance to serve self-interest without fear of retribution? A shocking question, with a built-in anti-climax; it cannot be answered.

To begin with this new appraisal of the two men and the circumstances of their flight, we must look first at the official story as outlined in the White Paper issued belatedly and as a result of pressure. And if this implies that the official story is not accurate or factual, there are no apologies. Rarely can a White Paper have been published which was so dishonest—not in what it actually said, but in what it concealed. Here are its first 23 Sections.

REPORT

CONCERNING THE DISAPPEARANCE OF TWO
FORMER FOREIGN OFFICE OFFICIALS

London, September 1955

On the evening of Friday, May 25, 1951, Mr. Donald Duart Maclean, a Counsellor in the senior branch of the Foreign Service and at that time Head of the American Department of the Foreign Office, and Mr. Guy Frances de Moncy Burgess, a Second Secretary in the junior branch of the Foreign Service, left the United Kingdom from Southampton on the boat for St. Malo. The circumstances of their departure from England, for which they had not sought sanction, were such as to make it obvious that they had deliberately fled the country. Both officers were suspended from duty on June 1, 1951, and their appointments in the Foreign Office were terminated on June 1, 1952, with effect from June 1, 1951.

2. Maclean was the son of a former Cabinet Minister, Sir Donald Maclean. He was born in 1913 and was educated at Gresham's School, Holt, and Trinity College, Cambridge, where he had a distinguished academic record. He successfully competed for the Diplomatic Service in 1935, and was posted in the first instance to the Foreign Office. He served subsequently in Paris, at Washington and in Cairo. He was an officer of exceptional ability and was promoted

21

to the rank of Counsellor at the early age of thirty-five. He was married to an American lady and had two young sons. A third child was born shortly after his disappearance.

3. In May 1950 while serving at His Majesty's Embassy, Cairo, Maclean was guilty of serious misconduct and suffered a form of breakdown which was attributed to overwork and excessive drinking. Until the breakdown took place his work had remained eminently satisfactory and there was no ground whatsoever for doubting his loyalty. After recuperation and leave at home he passed medically fit, and in October 1950 was appointed to be Head of the American Department of the Foreign Office which, since it does not deal with the major problems of Anglo-American relations, appeared to be within his capacity.

4. Since Maclean's disappearance a close examination of his background has revealed that during his student days at Cambridge from 1931 to 1934 he had expressed Communist sympathies, but there was no evidence that he had been a member of the Communist Party and indeed on leaving the University he had outwardly renounced his earlier Communist views.

5. Burgess was born in 1911 and was educated at the Royal Naval College, Dartmouth, at Eton and at Trinity College, Cambridge, where he had a brilliant academic record. After leaving Cambridge in 1935 he worked for a short time in London as a journalist and joined the B.B.C. in 1936 where he remained

until January 1939. From 1939 to 1941 he was employed in one of the war propaganda organisations. He rejoined the B.B.C. in 1941 and remained there until 1944 when he applied for and obtained a post as a temporary press officer in the News Department of the Foreign Office. He was not recruited into the Foreign Service through the open competitive examination but in 1947 took the opportunity open to temporary employees to present himself for establishment. He appeared before a Civil Service Commission Board and was recommended for the junior branch of the Foreign Service. His establishment took effect from January 1, 1947. He worked for a time in the office of the then Minister of State, Mr. Hector McNeil, and in the Far Eastern Department of the Foreign Office. In August 1950 he was transferred to Washington as a Second Secretary.

6. Early in 1950 the security authorities informed the Foreign Office that in late 1949 while on holiday abroad Burgess had been guilty of indiscreet talk about secret matters of which he had official knowledge. For this he was severely reprimanded. Apart from this lapse his service in the Foreign Office was up to the time of his appointment to Washington satisfactory and there seemed good reason to hope that he would make a useful career.

7. In Washington, however, his work and behaviour gave rise to complaint. The Ambassador reported that his work had been unsatisfactory in that he lacked thoroughness and balance in routine matters,

that he had come to the unfavourable notice of the Department of State because of his reckless driving and that he had had to be reprimanded for carelessness in leaving confidential papers unattended. The Ambassador requested that Burgess be removed from Washington and this was approved. He was recalled to London in early May 1951 and was asked to resign from the Foreign Service. Consideration was being given to the steps that would be taken in the event of his refusing to do so. It was at this point that he disappeared.

8. Investigations into Burgess's past have since shown that he, like Maclean, went through a period of Communist leanings while at Cambridge and that he too on leaving the University renounced his views. No trace can be found in his subsequent career of direct participation in the activities of Left-Wing organisations; indeed he was known after leaving Cambridge to have had some contact with organisations such as the Anglo-German Club.

9. The question has been asked whether the association of these two officers with each other did not give rise to suspicion. The fact is that although we have since learned that Maclean and Burgess were acquainted during their undergraduate days at Cambridge, they gave no evidence during the course of their career in the Foreign Service of any association other than would be normal between two colleagues. When Burgess was appointed to the Foreign Office Maclean was in Washington and at the time Burgess

himself was appointed to Washington Maclean was back in the United Kingdom awaiting assignment to the American Department in the Foreign Office. It is now clear that they were in communication with each other after the return of Burgess from Washington in 1951 and they may have been in such communication earlier. Their relations were, however, never such as to cause remark.

10. In January 1949 the security authorities received a report that certain Foreign Office information had leaked to the Soviet authorities some years earlier. The report amounted to little more than a hint and it was at the time impossible to attribute the leak to any particular individual. Highly secret but widespread and protracted enquiries were begun by the security authorities and the field of suspicion had been narrowed by mid-April 1951 to two or three persons.

By the beginning of May Maclean had come to be regarded as the principal suspect. There was, however, even at that time, no legally admissible evidence to support a prosecution under the Official Secrets Acts. Arrangements were made to ensure that information of exceptional secrecy and importance should not come into his hands. In the meantime the security authorities arranged to investigate his activities and contacts in order to increase their background knowledge and if possible to obtain information which could be used as evidence in a prosecution. On May 25 the then Secretary of State, Mr. Herbert

Morrison, sanctioned a proposal that the security authorities should question Maclean. In reaching this decision it had to be borne in mind that such questioning might produce no confession or voluntary statement from Maclean sufficient to support a prosecution but might serve only to alert him and to reveal the nature and the extent of the suspicions against him. In that event he would have been free to make arrangements to leave the country and the authorities would have had no legal power to stop him. Everything therefore depended on the interview and the security authorities were anxious to be fully prepared as was humanly possible. They were also anxious that Maclean's house at Tatsfield, Kent, should be searched and this was an additional reason for delaying the proposed interview until mid-June when Mrs. Maclean who was then pregnant was expected to be away from home.

11. It is now clear that in spite of the precautions taken by the authorities Maclean must have been aware, at some time before his disappearance, that he was under investigation. One explanation may be that he observed that he was no longer receiving certain types of secret papers. It is also possible that he detected that he was under observation. Or he may have been warned. Searching enquiries involving interrogations were made into this last possibility. Insufficient evidence was obtainable to form a definite conclusion or to warrant prosecution.

12. Maclean's absence did not become known to

the authorities until the morning of Monday, May 28. The Foreign Office is regularly open for normal business on Saturday mornings but officers can from time to time obtain leave to take a week-end off. In accordance with this practice Maclean applied for and obtained leave to be absent on the morning of Saturday, May 26. His absence therefore caused no remark until the following Monday morning when he failed to appear at the Foreign Office. Burgess was on leave and under no obligation to report his movements.

13. Immediately the flight was known all possible action was taken in the United Kingdom, and the French and other Continental security authorities were asked to trace the whereabouts of the fugitives and if possible to intercept them. All the British Consulates in Western Europe were alerted and special efforts were made to discover whether the fugitives had crossed the French frontiers on May 26 or 27. As a result of these and other enquiries it was established that Maclean and Burgess together left Tatsfield by car for Southampton in the late evening of Friday, May 25, arrived at Southampton at midnight, caught the s.s. *Falaise* for St. Malo and disembarked at that port at 11.45 the following morning, leaving suitcases and some of their clothing on board. They were not seen on the train from St. Malo to Paris and it has been reported that the two men, believed to be Maclean and Burgess, took a taxi to Rennes and got there the 1.18 p.m. train to Paris. Nothing more was seen of them.

14. Since the disappearance various communications have been received from other members of their families. On June 7, 1951, telegrams ostensibly from Maclean were received by his mother Lady Maclean, and his wife Mrs. Melinda Maclean, who were both at the time in the United Kingdom. The telegram to Lady Maclean was a short personal message, signed by a nickname known only within the immediate family circle. It merely stated that all was well. That addressed to Mrs. Maclean was similar, expressing regret for the unexpected departure and was signed "Donald". Both telegrams were despatched in the evening of June 6. Their receipt was at once reported to the security authorities, but it was impossible to identify the person or persons who had handed them in. The original telegraph forms showed, however, that the messages had been written in a hand which was clearly not Maclean's. The character of the handwriting, and some misspelling, suggested that both telegrams had been written by a foreigner.

15. On June 7, 1951, a telegram was received in London by Mrs. Bassett, Burgess's mother. It contained a short and affectionate personal message, together with a statement that the sender was embarking on a long Mediterranean holiday, and was ostensibly from Burgess himself. The telegram had been handed in at a Post Office in Rome earlier on the day of its receipt. As with the telegrams from Paris to Maclean's family, there was no possibility of

identifying the person who had handed it in. The handwriting had the appearance of being foreign and was certainly not that of Burgess.

16. According to information given to the Foreign Office in confidence by Mrs. Dunbar, Maclean's mother-in-law, who was then living with her daughter at Tatsfield, she received on August 3, 1951, two registered letters posted in St. Gallen, Switzerland, on August 1. One contained a draft on the Swiss Bank Corporation, London, for the sum of £1,000 payable to Mrs. Dunbar; the other, a draft payable to Mrs. Dunbar for the same sum, drawn by the Union Bank of Switzerland on the Midland Bank, 122 Old Broad Street, London. Both drafts were stated to have been remitted by order of a Mr. Becker, whose address was given as the Hotel Central, Zurich. Exhaustive enquiries in collaboration with the Swiss authorities have not led to the identification of Mr. Becker and it is possible that the name given was false.

17. Shortly after the receipt of these bank drafts Mrs. Maclean received a letter in her husband's handwriting. It had been posted in Reigate, Surrey, on August 5, 1951, and was of an affectionate, personal nature as from husband to wife. It gave no clue as to Maclean's whereabouts or the reason for his disappearance but it explained that the bank drafts, which for convenience had been sent to Mrs. Dunbar, were intended for Mrs. Maclean.

18. Lady Maclean received a further letter from

her son, on August 15, 1951. There is no doubt that it was in his own handwriting. It had been posted at Herne Hill on August 11.

19. Mrs. Bassett, the mother of Burgess, received a letter in Burgess's handwriting on December 22, 1953. The letter was personal and gave no information as to Burgess's whereabouts. It was simply dated "November" and had been posted in South-East London on December 21. The last message received from either of the two men was a further letter from Burgess to his mother which was delivered in London on December 25, 1954. This letter was also personal and disclosed nothing of Burgess's whereabouts. It too was simply dated "November". It had been posted in Poplar, E.14, on December 23.

20. On September 11, 1953, Mrs. Maclean, who was living in Geneva, left there by car with her three children. She told her mother who was staying with her that she had unexpectedly come across an acquaintance whom she and her husband had previously known in Cairo and who had invited her and the children to spend a week-end with him at Territet, near Montreux. She stated that she would return to Geneva on September 13 in time for the two elder children to attend school the following day. By September 14 her mother, alarmed at her failure to return, reported the matter to Her Majesty's Consul-General in Geneva and also by telephone to London. Security officers were at once despatched to Geneva where they placed themselves at the disposal of the Swiss

Police who were already making intensive enquiries. On the afternoon of September 16, Mrs. Maclean's car was found in a garage in Lausanne. She had left it on the afternoon of the 11th saying she would return for it in a week. The garage hand who reported this added that Mrs. Maclean had proceeded with her children to the Lausanne railway station. On the same day, September 16, Mrs. Dunbar reported to the Geneva police the receipt of a telegram purporting to have come from her daughter. The telegram explained that Mrs. Maclean had been delayed "owing to unforeseen circumstances" and asked Mrs. Dunbar to inform the school authorities that the two elder children would be returning in a week. Mrs. Maclean's youngest child was referred to in this telegram by a name known only to Mrs. Maclean, her mother and other intimates. The telegram had been handed in at the Post Office in Territet at 10.58 that morning by a woman whose description did not agree with that of Mrs. Maclean. The handwriting on the telegram form was not Mrs. Maclean's and it showed foreign characteristics similar to those in the telegrams received in 1951 by Lady Maclean and Mrs. Bassett.

21. From information subsequently received from witnesses in Switzerland and Austria, it seems clear that the arrangements for Mrs. Maclean's departure from Geneva had been carefully planned, and that she proceeded by train from Lausanne on the evening of September 11, passing the Swiss-Austrian frontier that night, and arriving at Schwarzach St. Viet in the

American Zone of Austria at approximately 9.15 on the morning of September 12. The independent evidence of a porter at Schwarzach, St. Viet and of witnesses travelling on the train has established that she left the train at this point. Further evidence, believed to be reliable, shows that she was met at the station by an unknown man driving a car bearing Austrian number-plates. The further movements of this car have not been traced. It is probable that it took Mrs. Maclean and the children from Schwarzach St. Viet to neighbouring territory in Russian occupation whence she proceeded on her journey to join her husband.

22. There was no question of preventing Mrs. Maclean from leaving the United Kingdom to go to live in Switzerland. Although she was under no obligation to report her movements, she had been regularly in touch with the security authorities, and had informed them that she wished to make her home in Switzerland. She gave two good reasons, firstly that she wished to avoid the personal embarrassment to which she had been subjected by the Press in the United Kingdom, and secondly, that she wished to educate her children in the International School in Geneva. It will be remembered that Mrs. Maclean was an American citizen and in view of the publicity caused by her husband's flight it was only natural that she should wish to bring up her children in new surroundings. Before she left for Geneva the security authorities made arrangements with her whereby

she was to keep in touch with the British authorities in Berne and Geneva in case she should receive any further news from her husband or require advice or assistance. Mrs. Maclean was a free agent. The authorities had no legal means of detaining her in the United Kingdom. Any form of surveillance abroad would have been unwarranted.

23. In view of the suspicions held against Maclean and of the conspiratorial manner of his flight, it was assumed, though it could not be proved, that his destination and that of his companion must have been the Soviet Union or some other territory behind the Iron Curtain. Now Vladimir Petrov, the former Third Secretary of the Soviet Embassy in Canberra who sought political asylum on April 3, 1954, has provided confirmation of this. Petrov himself was not directly concerned in the case and his information was obtained from conversation with one of his colleagues in Soviet service in Australia. Petrov states that both Maclean and Burgess were recruited as spies for the Soviet Government while students at University, with the intention that they should carry out their esponiage tasks in the Foreign Office, and that in 1951, by means unknown to him, one or other of the two men became aware that their activities were under investigation.

3

The Great Debate

THE CONSPIRACY came after the crime. When Guy
Burgess and Donald Maclean fled Britain on that night in
May, they knew what they were doing; they knew where
they were going. But they could never have dreamed of
the extraordinary consequences they were leaving
behind.

They left behind them a trail of fear, suspicion, lies,
deceit and evasion. A bewildered nation learned of
their action eleven days after the event—and in that time
the conspiracy was born. It exists to this day. The public
wanted the truth; it has not been told, even now.

The object of the belated White Paper was to put an
end to the doubt, dismay and disquiet at home and
abroad. It did not succeed.

To gauge the measure of its failure and the weight of
conspiracy and collusion, it is helpful to read the
opinion of *The Times*, which might have been expected
to mend the broken fences of the Establishment. Instead,
this appeared, under the heading of "Too Little and
Too Late":

" 'Two points call for comment' says the White
Paper on Maclean and Burgess. That is typical of its
primness and defensiveness. There are not two but a

dozen points that call for comment, and the White Paper throws little new light on them.

"Appearing as it does, scandalously late, four and a quarter years after the two men fled the country, the White Paper might have been expected to give many details hitherto unknown. It does, indeed, mention that Burgess had, just before his flight, been specifically asked to resign from the Foreign Office because of reckless and careless conduct while posted in the United States. It also discloses that on May 25th, 1951, the very day of the two men's disappearance, the Foreign Secretary at the time (Mr. Morrison) agreed that Maclean should be questioned by the security authorities because of suspicions that he had previously passed Foreign Office information over to the Soviet authorities. For some unaccountable reason these facts were not made known until now.

"For the rest, the Paper does little more than confirm a good part of the information already known through the Press, and especially through the disclosures of Mr. Petrov in Australia. There is very little doubt that, but for the knowledge that Mr. Petrov was going to make his information public, the Foreign Office and the security authorities would not have decided to publish a White Paper at all, even now.

"Throughout the past four and quarter years the pattern has been invariably the same. A Press report has been followed by a reluctant and often tendentious admission in the House or at the Foreign Office.

35

Official statements were made which are now seen to be misleading. No doubt the spokesmen themselves were put up without the proper information which is usual on foreign affairs. Even so, it is hard to square the suggestion, a year ago, that Petrov's evidence was simply based on hearsay, and was 'to be treated with some reserve' with the White Paper's admission that Petrov has 'provided confirmation' of parts of the story.

"An even stranger discrepancy exists between the White Paper's evidence that Maclean was being watched on suspicion of passing information to the Russians, and Lord Reading's statement to the Lords on October 28th, 1952. 'Mr. Maclean,' said Lord Reading, 'performed his official duties satisfactorily up to the day of his disappearance.' The White Paper defends what it coyly calls the 'reticence of Ministerial replies' on the grounds that it is not desirable at any moment to let the other side know how much has been discovered or guess at the means used to discover it. An excellent principle, but how does it apply in this case? The Foreign Office needed no elaborate means to 'discover' that it had asked Burgess to resign or that it was closely watching Maclean; and the Russians already knew—otherwise they would not have helped the two men to escape.

"The net result of 'reticence' was the opposite of that intended. Instead of becoming bored with the affair, the public scented a mystery and wondered uneasily how much was being hidden.

"The White Paper does little to remove doubts about the security authorities' handling of the matter. It says that once suspicions fastened on to Maclean, they took a calculated risk that he became aware of their watch and made tracks for abroad. Events showed that they calculated wrongly; he did escape. But it is more extraordinary to read that, although gravely suspecting him, they decided not to keep a watch on his house in Kent. More extraordinary still, on the very day that authority was given to question him, he was allowed to go from London (where he was watched) on leave to Kent (where he was not watched). And, according to the White Paper, his flight that same evening, May 25th, 'did not become known to the authorities until the morning of Monday, May 28th'. They had cut themselves off from all means of knowing.

"Another point, less serious but no less bewildering, is that the White Paper says that the two men left the country 'when the security authorities were on their track'. Was Burgess, then, also being watched? There is nothing else in the White Paper to suggest it. The evidence produced is simply that he had been asked to resign after the Ambassador in Washington had reported on his personal behaviour. The authorities cannot have it both ways. If there was suspicion of espionage in this case the evidence should be in the White Paper. If the authorities had no such suspicions, they evidently had been caught napping. The mystery is deepened by the Foreign

Office statement that it was now believed that both men were 'long-term agents' for the Soviet Union. Petrov has said so, and his testimony is accepted, but on British evidence the part of Burgess has not been brought to light.

"Equally unsatisfactory is the way in which the White Paper deals with the manner in which the two men were kept for so long in the Foreign Service. All questions of spying apart, their personal behaviour at times should have raised far stronger and earlier questionings about their suitability for responsible work. Stories of their riotous bouts were common talk in London. Were these men to be trusted with State secrets? Did the authorities go on to ask what was the root cause of the evident strains which the two men were under? It is good to be reminded in the White Paper that, since the disappearance of the two men, security in the Foreign Service has been tightened and that more searching enquiries are now made into the characters and antecedents of candidates and members. The whole affair calls for full, honest scrutiny before the forum of Parliament; and there must be no disposition, as there has been on previous occasions, to score party points. The record of the Foreign Service is second to none for steadfastness, hard work and loyalty, but the House will have searching and important questions to ask."

Where *The Times* led the uproar for the moment, the others were not far behind.

The *Daily Telegraph* called the White Paper "a total failure", the *Daily Mail*, "alarming", the *News Chronicle*, "laughable, were the whole thing not so serious". The *New Statesman* declared that "the White Paper reveals nothing but incompetence".

Richard Crossman in the *Daily Mirror* wrote that it "makes it clear that many of the answers which Ministers were briefed to give were deliberate suppressions of the truth—and some were actual lies".

The *Daily Express* asked, simply: "Who are the guilty men?"

When the Foreign Secretary, Mr. Harold Macmillan, rose to open the debate in the House of Commons, he faced a grave and critical audience. His opening phrase showed that he himself had not underestimated the gravity of the question.

"It can rarely have happened in Parliamentary history," he said, "that a Secretary of State should have to unfold such a painful story for consideration." Then he sketched briefly the history of the torn loyalties of the thirties, particularly the divisions of opinion brought about by the Spanish Civil War and largely ending in the Stalin-Hitler Pact "for the duration". But, at the end of the war, the clash of loyalties was revived.

"Thus it was," he said, "that men could be found in Britain who could put the interests of another country before their own and commit the horrible crime of treachery."

This occurred not only among criminals and degenerates, but in men holding high technical and scientific posts, in men of philosophic and literary attainments, and finally in the Foreign Service.

Many who had seen that service at work at home and abroad, he went on, would agree that Britain was fortunate to have a service of the highest quality, giving loyal and devoted service to the Crown and the nation. That Foreign Service regarded the severe blow against its reputation as a personal case which had caused a profound shock to Parliament and the general public.

It was an unexceptionable opening, and the tribute to the Foreign Service brought the first Hear Hears. Mr. Macmillan now had to get down to cases, and he began with the security services.

He made it clear that Ministers, both past and present, who were connected with the Foreign Office must bear responsibility. He made the point that the "amateur" foreign service security men often had outside experience in this field, though he did not enlarge on this statement. He also said that he was not attracted by a secret police system in which everyone, high or low, should be followed about.

Although he said he did not complain of the criticisms made concerning the lack of precautionary measures in this case, Mr. Macmillan emphasised something which is still relevant today:

"Action against employees, whether of the State or anybody else, arising from suspicion and not from proof, might be taken with good motives. But, judging from what has happened in some other countries, I suggest that the practice might soon degenerate into the satisfaction of personal vendettas or a general system of tyranny, all in the name of public safety."

Next, he dealt with the two men themselves. First, Maclean. A difference had to be drawn between him and Burgess, he said, because Maclean entered the diplomatic service before the war by competitive examination in which he showed conspicuous ability. He was given an exceptionally good report, and no mention was made of his left-wing activities. Macmillan asked: "If the selection board had known that he expressed Communist sympathies as an undergraduate in those days, would the House feel that such a man should automatically be excluded from the public service?" Of course, the Opposition members cried "No".

He went on: "Surely it would have been regarded as one of the aberrations of youth which he might have been expected to live down?" It was a nice touch; the House relaxed with a ripple of laughter.

Then he made a curious and—in the light of later information—controversial point; until, and even after, Maclean's appointment in Cairo, his work was not only good but outstanding. "During the first fourteen years of his service there was no adverse comment," he said. The first sign of a breakdown—though it was a big one—had come in Cairo, as the House was to hear more fully, later.

Next came a rather delicate subject, and the Foreign Secretary put the facts baldly: "It is easy to be wise after the event, but at the end of five months' medical treatment he was put at the head of the American department. The appointment implied no promotion for him, and provided an opportunity to watch his conduct and his health."

Parliamentary eyebrows were raised, but Macmillan went on to deal with the position of Sir Roger Makins, formerly Maclean's immediate chief and later Ambassador in Washington. He was not in any way responsible for the conduct of an enquiry, nor had he been responsible for checking or clearing Maclean.

Now, Guy Burgess. This man, he said, was first taken on as temporary Press officer in 1944, and his career previously had seemed respectable enough. In 1945 he applied for Establishment in the junior branch of the Foreign Office, and a board of appointment was impressed by his academic qualifications, reports from the news department and the B.B.C. They did not know that he had been "unsatisfactory" in one of the B.B.C. departments.

In Washington, however, said Macmillan, Burgess was a failure. "The Ambassador reported unfavourably both on his office work and his behaviour outside, and in May 1951, four years after his establishment and nine months after his appointment in Washington, he was recalled and the conclusion reached that he would have to leave the service.

"Until the day of his disappearance there were no grounds for suspecting that he was working against the security of the State. He had been indiscreet, but then indiscretion is not generally the characteristic of a secret agent."

Macmillan returned to the question of security checks,

42

which was to become an important issue. The disappearance of Burgess and Maclean, he said, had already forced one major change in security regulations. From 1945 until 1951 there had been a "negative" check on persons entering government service. But this was simply a check with government files to discover whether the applicant had already been in trouble with the security services, the police or any other department. "Positive" vetting started in 1951 and entailed a search of the applicant's career, from school through all his previous employers. In the years between then and the debate 900 Foreign Office cases had been vetted in this way. Four men had been sacked and six transferred.

Mr. Macmillan had given a masterly performance on very thin ice. When he finally sat down he had the satisfaction of knowing that he had indeed presented the case in the best possible light, with the strong inference that if things had not been all that they should have been in the past, then things would certainly be very much better in the future.

Many Members on both sides of the House, however, were highly critical of the security services, and of the Foreign Office. Mr. Herbert Morrison commanded particular interest when he rose; he had, after all, been Foreign Secretary at the time. "There must be an enquiry," he said. "The country will not be satisfied without an enquiry of some sort and covering an adequate field, for the country has a right to know that action is being taken arising out of an experience which is disturbing and worrying to us all."

The Prime Minister, Sir Anthony Eden, wound up by replying that if it was a question of the police wanting to hold people indefinitely while they collected evidence against them, he would never be Prime Minister of a government that asked those powers of the House. This was a sentiment that brought an easy round of applause. He then pushed the point further:

"Before the limitations of the existing law are relaxed, Parliament will have to weigh carefully the balance of advantage and disadvantage. For it would be tragedy indeed if we were to destroy our freedom in the effort to preserve it."

So the delicate subject of liberty, to which the House is always rightfully sensitive, was used to side-track the real issue of the debate, which was: what went wrong? And who was to blame?

To find out we must look carefully at the backgrounds and the friends of Burgess and Maclean.

4

Burgess, the Background

It is perhaps hard, in the light of subsequent events, to imagine and understand the mood of the 1930s.

It was the decade during which Hitler rose to power on the back of a new European ideology. From the Japanese invasion of Manchuria in 1931 until the appeasers faced facts in September 1939 the years were punctuated by a succession of decisions and events which were hotly (and, one is tempted to think perhaps, more intelligently) debated amongst the young post-war generation of intellectuals than in the Houses of Parliament, where our legislators were going through one of the least inspired phases in their history.

They were the years, too, of hunger marches at home, of three million unemployed, of pathetic queues for the dole and the heady atmosphere of the "intellectuals' war" in Spain where some of the most brilliant young men of the generation lost their lives in an effort to give practical support to the ideas about which they were so articulate.

It was against this background that both Donald Maclean and Guy Burgess went up to Cambridge. Much has been made of the family background of the two men in an effort to prove this or that theory of genetics. The truth of the matter is that at that stage their backgrounds could not have been more normal, or typical of the university undergraduates of the 1930s.

Donald's father died during his first year at Cambridge. He had been a distinguished politician. Knighted for his political services, he had been a one-time Liberal Cabinet Minister and later Chairman of the group of Independent Liberals in the House of Commons known as the "Wee Frees".

The relatively slender Maclean fortunes did not run to an Eton education. Instead Donald went to a minor Public School, Gresham's School at Holt, where his academic record was just good enough to warrant the expense of a university.

He went up to Trinity Hall in 1931 with an allowance which left nothing over for luxurious living. At eighteen he was a serious-minded young man, with little small talk and no taste for the sybaritic fripperies which so appealed to Burgess. Perhaps there was more than a touch of the Scottish Calvinist in his make-up.

Guy's family, being in a rather more comfortable financial bracket, sent him first to Eton and then, when he developed an ambition for a Naval career, to Dartmouth. A suggestion made by a journalist in later years (and repeated, unchecked, by others) that he was sacked from Dartmouth for stealing is quite untrue. His eyesight was found to be defective and F. W. Dobbs, his old house-master, arranged for him to return to Eton—not an easy thing to achieve.

His career at Eton was, if anything, above average. He was in the sixth form and second among the Oppidans.

The opinion of the then Headmaster of Eton, given in 1928 shortly after Guy's return from Dartmouth, is interesting. He wrote:

"At the moment his ideas are running away with him, and he is finding in verbal quibbles and Chestertonian comparisons a rather unhealthy delight, but he is such a sane person, and so modest essentially that I do not feel this very much matters. The great thing is that he really thinks for himself. It is refreshing to find one who is really well read and who can become enthusiastic or have something to say about most things from Vermeer to Meredith. He is also a lively and amusing person, generous, I think, and very good natured. He should do very well."

Because of the Dartmouth interlude, Burgess was already a year older than his term by the time he went up to Cambridge in 1930. He was to read history in which he had won an open scholarship to Trinity College. Donald Maclean, whom he was to meet there for the first time, was reading Modern Languages at Trinity Hall. It would have needed second sight indeed to foretell, when the two men first met, probably at a party in somebody's rooms or, casually, in a bar with other friends, that, one day, their names would be linked together in the public mind as firmly as Livingstone and Stanley. For almost from the outset their careers were to take on a different guise. At Cambridge Donald Maclean pursued outwardly a course of undistinguished competence, culminating in a solid second-class degree, and passed into the Foreign Office somewhere over half-way down the list.

Not so Burgess. Almost immediately he became wholly and completely absorbed in all the more exotic aspects of university life. True, he joined the Pitt Club, the status symbol of the horsier and more conventional-minded undergraduates, but all his other extra-mural activities were soon to single him out as one of the most talked-about undergraduates of his time.

To begin with, he was what one can only describe as a "dedicated" homosexual. So much has been hinted at in relation to this subject about both Burgess and Maclean that it is probably, at the outset, as well to put their "deviationism" in this respect in its correct perspective.

Burgess was not only entirely homosexual but made not the slightest attempt to conceal it. Rather he flaunted it, pursuing men with all the unabashed enthusiasm of a Piccadilly prostitute. Not only were his affairs legion, but he managed, by some strange power of personality, to keep his discarded lovers as friends long after he had lost interest in them sexually.

Because of his brash, open approach he had a very considerable measure of success, far greater than the more inhibited homosexuals who try to satisfy their desires with the veiled approach and the carefully dropped hint.

Maclean was one of Guy Burgess's conquests, or so Burgess boasted to a mutual friend in later years, and there seems to be no reasonable doubt to this claim in view of subsequent events. On the other hand Maclean was not at all the sort of person one might expect to have homosexual tendencies. The two men could hardly have been less alike in temperament. Burgess, the brash, opinionative extrovert, ever ready with the apt epigram and devastating turn of phrase, contrasted oddly with the almost austere characteristics of Maclean.

Maclean presented a strictly conformist exterior to the world. Realising that he could never have the verbal agility of Burgess, he did not indulge in small talk and, unless he had had a lot to drink, rarely gave an opinion without appearing to give the matter a lot of thought. Yet according to those who knew him at the time he was very much under the influence of the volatile Burgess.

Exactly at what point Burgess came into contact with the Communist Party will never be known. All that is certain is that it was soon after he came up and that, in his second year, he was already a fully-fledged member. Much has been made of these early associations with the Communist Party and considerable criticism levelled against Burgess's future employers that they did not enquire more closely into his political background during his Cambridge days. Certainly, and typically, Burgess himself made no attempt to disguise his views or to refrain from giving practical expression to them.

In his capacity as a member of the Anti-War Movement he took an extremely active part, for example, in an Armistice Day demonstration which can have done little to raise his stock with his fellow members of the Pitt Club. On this occasion Burgess and a group of fellow-pacifists decided, as part of a general pacifist demonstration, to lay a wreath on the Cambridge War Memorial, inscribed "In memory of the victims of an imperialist war which was not of their making". The attempt was strongly resisted by another section of undergraduates and it was only as a result of the most warlike action that the pacifists were able to achieve their objective.

Burgess also managed to get himself involved, as many undergraduates have before and since, in well-meaning efforts to improve the lot of the College servants by inducing them to corporate action—and with as little success.

The subjects of his good intentions were the Hall waiters at Trinity, a section of the long-suffering but reasonably contented army of servants who, since time immemorial, have been the passing cause of the first stirrings of social conscience in successive generations of undergraduates. On this occasion matters got so far as the threatening of strike action but history does not record how, this time, the College authorities dealt with the perennial situation.

There was another incident worth mentioning. With others he joined in booing Neville Chamberlain, who was speaking as guest of honour at the Founder's Feast at Trinity, when the then Chancellor of the Exchequer claimed that although there were then two million unemployed, there was no real hardship being suffered by the men and their families.

But there must be few undergraduates who do not

have a similar repertoire of youthful deeds of bravado, and these incidents hardly read like the early days of a devoted revolutionary.

Perhaps his general attitude to these matters is most easily understood by the description of the part he played in the hunger marches of 1934 as told by Tom Driberg in the profile he wrote of Guy Burgess as a result of visiting him in Moscow.

"In the Cambridge of those days," Driberg writes, "Socialist and Communist undergraduates had many opportunities of demonstrating their opposition to the existing order. One was provided by the hunger march of 1934. With some undergraduates, Guy went to Huntingdon to meet the marchers, marched with them to Cambridge, and then went to London by train, to meet them again and march with them to Hyde Park."

One cannot really feel that this leisurely, almost patronising participation in one of the great tragedies of the time amounted to much more than a boyish lark calculated to enhance his reputation for left-wing intellectualism at the University, rather than to provide a real inspiration for the marchers. Certainly few present-day Ban-the-Bomb demonstrators would expect to be taken very seriously on such a low mileage!

But beneath this rather tiresomely naïve exterior another side to the complex personality which was Guy Burgess was already beginning to take shape.

There is no doubt that Burgess, during his university career, showed signs of brilliance and may well have fallen not far short of Geronwy Rees's description of him as "the most brilliant undergraduate of his time". Although, in his third year, he suffered a severe nervous breakdown, which resulted in his taking only an aegrotat degree, no less a personage than Dr. G. M. Trevelyan urged both on Burgess and Pembroke that he should become a Fellow of the College.

Cyril Connolly cites as further evidence of his brilliance that he was one of the half-dozen or so undergraduates invited to join that most selective of all secret societies, the Society of the Apostles. It is likely however that membership of this rather pretentious-sounding body, which has been in existence for over a hundred years, and prides itself on its sense of brotherhood and the "utmost intimacy" into which its members at once fall, was a tribute to Guy Burgess's physical rather than purely mental attributes.

Perhaps Guy Burgess's most striking characteristic was the quite remarkable personal influence he was able to exert on those who came into contact with him. It is true that he chose his friends, rather than was chosen by them, and that by far the majority of them were practising homosexuals, but it does not alter the fact that he was endowed with personal qualities of charm which enabled him to make friends easily.

It is also undoubtedly true that he used his talents in this direction quite shamelessly to achieve his own ends. To quote his own words, talking to Tom Driberg again, he exploited his advantages "cynically and consciously".

Had it not been for this unusual degree of amorality, which, typically, Guy Burgess made to seem almost one of his most charming traits, it is quite likely that he would have been able to shed this Communist phase, as did so many others, when he went down from the University. Oxford and Cambridge had been the happy hunting ground of the British Communist Party in the 1930s, to a degree which they have never since achieved. For most undergraduates it was an ephemeral experience which was not taken too seriously by the Communist Party itself.

Guy Burgess was, however, another cup of tea altogether, and there is little doubt that he was recognised as such soon after he joined the Party. With his extrovert personality and his ability to influence people and his genuine intellectual interest in Marxism he was of much more potential value than the wishy-washy introverts who were usually attracted to the cause.

Anyway, within a short time of joining, Burgess had ceased to be an intellectual moth fluttering round a mildly exciting candle, but had become very much part of the candle itself. It is typical of his nature that he not only was pathologically unable to keep anything which interested him to himself, but had a compulsion to influence other people with his own opinions and doctrines. This, coupled with his passion to impress his male conquests, made him a natural recruiting agent for the party and this is the role which he assumed within a few months of joining.

Moreover it is unlikely that this was a role given to him by whoever had recruited him for the Communist Party. It is much more likely that such promising material had been passed over to the Comintern, the Communist international organisation, which would be quick to see the use to which his talents were best suited.

It is likely, too, that it was the Comintern which dictated the next move in his political development.

In 1934 Burgess went to Moscow.

This was not, as one might imagine, a move suggested to him from inside the Party. Indeed it is quite possible that they did not approve of it.

The trip arose out of discussions with his friend Geronwy Rees the previous summer. Rees, a Fellow of All Souls, Oxford, was one of Burgess's closest friends and one of the very few who were not homosexuals. His interest in Burgess dated from a casual meeting two years earlier when he detected in him the seeds of what he felt might well be one of the great minds of the generation. Moreover Rees was intensely interested in the practice and theory of Communism.

In the event Burgess made the trip but without Geronwy Rees, whose commitments prevented him at the last moment from accompanying him. Instead Burgess went with the well-known Oxford Communist and expert in Marxism Derek Blaikie, who was later to die in the war.

There are two views of the outcome of the trip. Rees holds the view that, during the visit, Burgess met many leading Communists, including Nikolai Bukarin, and may well have been influenced at that time to play an active part as a Soviet spy. Burgess himself hotly denies this, claiming that he certainly did not meet Bukarin and that anyway, even if he had, it was wrong to read any sinister significance into it as Bukarin had not, as Rees claimed, anything to do with the Comintern.

Whatever the truth of the matter it was shortly after Burgess's return from Moscow that his friends noticed that his politics had undergone an apparent volte-face.

Whilst still paying lip service to the general concept of Communism, he started to claim that he himself had discovered some fundamental errors, not so much in its theory but in its practice.

"It was most strange," said a friend of his at that time. "One day everything in the Communist garden was lovely and the next he was preaching with every evidence of sincerity that Communism was in fact a reactionary movement and that the progressive forces were to be found on the extreme right."

In the middle of this neo-fascist stage Burgess suddenly decided to quit the Party. This he did with all the rolling of drums and fanfare of trumpets which it is so easy to achieve inside the tightly knit circle of a university. At the same time Donald Maclean announced that he, too, had renounced Communism. There had in fact hardly been a honeymoon for either of them as Party members before their marriage was declared over.

Shortly afterwards Maclean passed into the Foreign Office and, donning the striped trousers and stiff white collar of his trade, appeared to have left behind him for ever the amusing intellectual flirtations of his youth. It was also the last regular contact he was to have with

Burgess, until their names were to be on everybody's lips as "the Missing Diplomats".

What, in fact, was the significance of this University interlude in the light of the events which were to come?

The significance was real and far reaching. The period when Burgess and Maclean were at the University were most valuable years for the Communist Party. It was indeed the springtime of the Communist intellectuals. Some like John Cornford and David Haden-Guest were to be killed fighting in Spain, others like David Hedley, who had been captain of Eton and, at Cambridge, was brought into the Communist Party by Burgess, were to die or be killed in the Second World War.

Others went out into the world protesting that their Communist days were over. Many of these, however, still had valuable service to render to the cause. Men like Burgess and Maclean—and Alan Nunn-May, their friend and contemporary, who does not come into this story.

Were there others? Undoubtedly there were. But where they are now and what they are doing is still a seventy-five thousand dollar question.

From 1935 onwards the lives of Guy Burgess and Donald Maclean went in such opposing directions that it seemed unlikely that they would meet again other than by chance or purely social reasons. Because Burgess has been the main dramatis persona so far it will probably be tidier to follow his story through, so far as it is known, before dealing with Maclean who up to this point has played a less spectacular role.

It is probable that Burgess, had he been younger,

would have applied, like Maclean, to join the Foreign Office. By the time he left the University however he was already too old to take the Civil Service examination.

There were two alternatives which appealed to him—journalism or the B.B.C. He tried journalism first and, as a true son of the Establishment, selected *The Times* for his début. It was not a successful experiment. In fact it lasted a month. Then he was back on the labour market.

About this time there occurred rather an odd interlude, which is worth relating in that it throws a sidelight on the circle that Burgess moved in.

A friend—though never a close friend—at Cambridge had been Victor Rothschild (now Lord Rothschild) and so it was natural enough for Guy, with his facility for making use of acquaintances, to ask himself down to stay at Victor's house in the country. During this visit Burgess met Victor's mother, Mrs. Charles Rothschild, who was enormously impressed by what her son had told her of his friend's political insight and after listening to Guy's own summing up, over dinner, of world affairs as they affected parts of the world in which the Rothschild family had financial interests, became in fact so impressed that she dispensed with the advice of the family banking house in the City and paid Guy Burgess a retainer of £100 a month to advise her on her personal investments, a list of which she gave him.

There is something rather piquant in the idea of Burgess, with his firmly held anti-capitalist beliefs, advising one of the richest women in the world on her investments.

Incidentally, with the worsening of the political situation in Europe, he at one stage advised Mrs. Rothschild to dispose of her European holdings and re-invest in America. Although she agreed with the soundness of the advice, she refused to take it on patriotic grounds; heartening sidelight on a field of interest not noted for allowing its heart to go to its head.

It was about this time, too, that Burgess took part in another expedition abroad—this time to Germany. The object of the trip was obscure and the composition of the party even more odd. Although they went under no known auspices, the diverse occupations of his companions would appear to give them few interests in common.

There was the elderly Colonel Macnamara, Conservative Member of Parliament, a clergyman in the person of the Ven. J. H. Sharp, who described himself as Archdeacon for South West Europe, and a young Civil Servant, Mr. Tom Wylie who was, at that time, private secretary to the Permanent Under Secretary of the War Office—and Guy Burgess.

Although Burgess subsequently refused to be drawn on any political aspects of his trip to Germany he took great delight in regaling his friends with hilarious accounts of the idiosyncrasies of his companions. Whatever brought the four of them together in the first place is hard to imagine.

For a time after his return Burgess took a job as personal secretary to Colonel Macnamara, who might be described, to put it mildly, as extremely right-wing in his political views. To friends who taxed Burgess with this seeming contradiction of everything in which he had expressed belief before, he would either make some vague remark to the effect that it was as well to understand every point of view, or go into a long diatribe purporting to explain that British Imperialist policy in India was the solution to world problems or some other equally unlikely thesis. It was only some years after this that he gave what seems to be the only plausible explanation of this period in his life to a man whom he regarded as one of his closest friends.

They were sitting together in the flat which Burgess then had near Ebury Street when he suddenly turned to his companion and said, very earnestly, with all the sincerity of the confessional box: "I want to tell you that I am a Comintern agent and have been ever since I left Cambridge."

Coming from anyone else but Burgess, with his known love of the theatrical and compulsive desire to shock people, it would have been an odd statement indeed. As it was, his friend did not take the remark too seriously. Instead he asked, if this were so, why he had been so obviously right-wing in his thinking since he had left the University. "Why not?" asked Burgess. "Why else do you think I left the Party and left Cambridge and took that absurd job with that ridiculous M.P? Did you really think I believed all that rigmarole about India and the Conservatives and the Nazis? But I had to invent something to say. The Party told me that I must break off all connection with them and as dramatically as possible, that I must quarrel with everyone I had known and try and start a political career of some kind. And I had to do it. So I did it. And all that nonsense served its purpose. Only I thought you were not taken in at the time by it. . . ."

The man to whom this statement was made did not quite know what to do about it. In the event he did nothing and Burgess never mentioned the subject again. Only after Burgess had disappeared did he go to M.I.5 and repeat the conversation which he had found at the time too improbable to credit.

Burgess did not stay long with his Tory M.P. Dr. G. M. Trevelyan, who had given up trying to persuade him that he should adopt an academic career, interceded with Sir Cecil Graves, a high official in the B.B.C., with the result that, after a short period of training Burgess found himself a member of the Talks Department.

Before long he found a niche that suited him well— anyhow for the time being. He was put in charge of a programme called "The Week in Westminster". His responsibility was to describe current affairs through the mouths of politicians of all parties in a week-by-week commentary on Parliamentary proceedings.

It was a job which gave him considerable scope for the exercise of his special talents. His ability to get on with people—and get things out of people—his quick grasp of the basic elements of a problem and his general political awareness enabled him to turn what could quite easily have been a dull and boring programme into an extremely popular one.

It was also an interesting job from his own point of

view in that it brought him into direct personal contact with a number of the leading political personalities of the day. Many of his most lasting friendships dated from this time.

Amongst other people whom he endeavoured to persuade to take part in the programme was Sir Winston Churchill, a man for whom he claimed to have a great personal admiration.

The interview took place at the time of the Czecho-slovak fiasco and the signing of the Russo-German pact. Burgess travelled to Chartwell to see Churchill and, although circumstances prevented Churchill taking part in the programme, he was obviously impressed with the young man who came to see him. One of Burgess's most prized possessions from then on was a copy of *Arms and the Covenant* inscribed "To Guy Burgess from Winston S. Churchill, to confirm his admirable sentiments. September 1938."

"When the war comes, as we both know it will," said Churchill (according to Burgess), as he gave him the book, "I have no doubt they will send for me. Come and see me and bring this book to remind me. I will find you a useful job to do."

Burgess, when the time did indeed arrive, did not take him up on his offer. He was too busy in other directions.

Burgess's life in London during his B.B.C. days was already beginning to assume the pattern which was, increasingly, to become his life. He was living then in a small, comfortable flat near Victoria which incorporated most of his ideas in interior decoration. The colour scheme was red, white and blue which, he claimed, was the only possible colour scheme one could ever live with, and the bedroom featured an enormous double bed with an Italianate bedhead. The bed indeed in all his successive flats was of such proportions as to dominate the whole apartment.

This description by a friend who visited him at this time gives a fascinating glimpse of his way of life.

"How well I remember going round to his flat one fine sunny morning that summer. This morning the patriotic décor was completely submerged in the indescribable debris and confusion of the party which had evidently taken place the night before. He was in bed, in his blue sheets beneath his red counterpane, littered with the Sunday newspapers. Beside his bed, on one side, stood a pile of books, which included *Middlemarch*, which he must have been reading for about the twentieth time, *Nicholas Nickleby*, Lady Gwendoline Cecil's *Life of Lord Salisbury*, Morley's *Gladstone* and Don Passos' *U.S.A.* These were all favourite books of his, which he read and re-read, with the faculty of discovering something new in them at each re-reading.

"On the other side of the bed stood two bottles of red wine and a very large, very heavy iron saucepan filled to the brim with a kind of thick grey gruel, a compound of porridge, kippers, bacon, garlic, onions and anything else that may have been lying about in his larder. This he had cooked the previous day, and on this he proposed to subsist to the following Monday. It contained, as he pointed out, everything which was necessary to sustain life, and what more could one require for intellectual happiness than the books which lay beside him on the other side?"

And there, for a blissful twenty-four hours he would lie, at intervals eating his gruel, dipping into his books and entertaining his friends.

His friends at this time, too, bear examination. There was the short, grossly-obese Kantz, who was said to have been with Bela Kun in Budapest and had just stopped being economic Editor of the news agency *Inprecorr*. There was a mysterious Englishman who conducted some sort of export/import agency in the Balkans and hurried round to see Burgess whenever he was in England. There was the usual "resident" boy which was a necessary concomitant to anywhere that Burgess lived. Like Oscar Wilde, Burgess preferred boys from the working class, whom he would have as house servants, bed fellows and chattels to lend to his friends. The current boy was called Jimmy, and was eventually passed on to a distinguished art critic by Burgess and replaced from his seemingly inexhaustible source of supply. It was one of his characteristics, and one perhaps which accounted for the hold he had over so many very important people, that he was not only deeply interested in his male friends' love affairs but acted as a procurer for them.

Another friend was a peculiarly detestable Frenchman

called Pfeiffer. Pfeiffer, like Kantz, was tough, cynical and experienced in the ways of the world. He was also greedy for power, money and sex. It was this seedy character, who looked as if the height of his ambition might be to keep a male brothel, who suddenly became *chef du Cabinet* to Daladier, then Prime Minister of France.

And, of course, there was von Putlitz. In a way he was the oddest of them all. Like the rest of them he was a homosexual, but unlike most of them, he was a man of great culture and intellect. The von Putlitz family of which he was the head, was one of the oldest and most powerful in Germany before the 1914 war.

Leaving the management of his estates to his younger brother, he entered the German Foreign Office. At the time Burgess already knew him. When he was appointed to a senior position under Ribbentrop in the German Embassy in London, he soon became one of his closest friends.

Whether Burgess had a hand in the matter or not will now probably never be known but the fact remains that one morning von Putlitz took a stroll across St. James's Park from the German Embassy in Carlton House Terrace for a meeting with Sir Robert Vansittart, later Lord Vansittart, but then Permanent Under Secretary at the Foreign Office. From that moment on von Putlitz joined the ranks of our spies. Dedicated to the destruction of the Hitler regime he reported every move inside the German Embassy at the time when Hitler was plotting with Ribbentrop the destruction of Britain.

There is a sequel to the von Putlitz story which may well have had its origins in those smoke-laden, heavy-drinking evenings in Burgess's garish flat. After the war, after holding several minor jobs in Western Germany, von Putlitz once again took a short walk—this time from West Berlin to East where he now works and lives.

One of the few people who have seen von Putlitz since is the well-known writer Sefton Delmer. To him he said: "It may well be that my friend Guy Burgess was influenced in his decision to go to Moscow by my example."

When this was suggested to Burgess, he readily agreed, adding: "I regard von Putlitz as one of the best and bravest men I have ever known."

It is quite within the bounds of credibility that Burgess, with his intense hatred of Nazism, was directly responsible for persuading von Putlitz to disaffect to the British side. If he did not, it is quite certain that he knew von Putlitz was working for us and, equally, that von Putlitz knew of Burgess's Communist affiliations, whatever they were.

There is another episode at this time which does not show Burgess in such a good light. It concerns the distasteful Pfeiffer.

Burgess was still advising Mrs. Rothschild and, in the course of his work for her, paid a number of visits to Paris. It was also at the time of the Czechoslovak crisis and Pfeiffer enlisted his aid to be a personal emissary between Daladier and Chamberlain. Although the letters were signed by subordinates it provided for a time a completely unofficial channel of communication between the two Premiers at a time when a complete understanding of each other's views, both official and unofficial was of the utmost importance.

Guy performed his role with his usual punctiliousness, omitting only to inform Pfeiffer (and of course the two principals involved), that he was having all the letters photostated before delivering them. This he had done by a man he used to meet at the St. Ermin's Hotel in Westminster.

These copies Burgess claims he passed on to an unofficial intelligence organisation and the only knowledge he had of their contents was when he was asked by the recipient to help him with translating them, as his own French was not very good. What he remembers of them he describes as "the communications of a panic-stricken patriot to an ignorant provincial ironmonger"—a typical example of the sort of meaningless generalisations with which he used to amuse and impress his friends.

The end of this affair, if Burgess's account of it (to Tom Driberg) is to be believed, is very odd indeed. At a vital stage in the proceedings Pfeiffer called Burgess to Paris to collect another communication. On this occasion however he seems not only to have known of the contents of the letter before delivering it—as usual, to be photographed—but to have disapproved of them. As Driberg puts it in his book:

"The letter insisted that Daladier was violently opposed to the Fleet mobilisation. But Guy had other information which indicated that this was not in fact

Daladier's own view, and that he had been forced by Bonnet and others of the Right to adopt it as part of the internal cabinet manœuvre. Guy, therefore, suppressed the letter."

At about the same time as this peculiar incident Henlein, the Czechoslovak Quisling, was on a visit to London and, by coincidence, stayed at an hotel where one of Burgess's young friends was working as a telephonist. Burgess arranged for this youth to make notes of all the calls made by Henlein and passed the information on to M.I.5.

These two examples of Burgess's activities are in fact very revealing of his nature. They show, for example, that he was insatiably curious and friends who knew him well confirm this trait. His curiosity was all-consuming and completely catholic in nature—rather like a jackdaw who has a compulsion to acquire anything that glitters irrespective of value.

The information which he obtained about Henlein's telephone calls can hardly have been of world-shaking importance, nor was it information which M.I.5 themselves could not have arranged to get had they thought it sufficiently worthwhile. Nonetheless Burgess could not resist taking advantage of the coincidence of having influence with his boy friend telephone operator to get in on the act.

The Pfeiffer episode, although on the face of it capable of a more sinister interpretation, was hardly of much more importance for, as Burgess himself remarks, the information was of such little importance that he has completely forgotten what the letters contained. Indeed it is likely that the whole importance of the letters has been blown up out of proportion, probably by Burgess himself, whose powers of exaggeration or of embroidering a good story are undoubted.

Although it has never been admitted, the recipient of this information acquired by such traditionally cloak-and-dagger methods was probably no more than a friend of Burgess's who was trying to hang together an intelligent news letter of the sort that is produced from time to time by people who claim to have inside information on a problem which happens to be in the public eye at the time.

Incidentally Burgess himself would have had a great future in the political newsletter field. There was no subject that you could mention, no personality you could name, but Burgess had some, usually disreputable, information which was not in the possession of anybody else. Moreover he retailed it with such conviction that even those who knew better were half-inclined to believe him.

All these incidents add up to little more than playing at boy scouts. Is there any evidence that underneath all these theatricals Burgess was playing a deeper game? There *is* one odd incident which seemed innocent enough to those who witnessed it at the time, but to which later events gave a sinister twist.

One Sunday morning Burgess rang a married couple and suggested meeting for lunch.

"I have got a personal letter to deliver in the East End, let's have lunch at ……… Chinese Restaurant," he suggested, naming a well-known East End restaurant which they both knew and had visited on many occasions.

When they arrived, Burgess excused himself for a moment and, crossing the road, put a letter through the box of a closed shop selling seamen's equipment and second-hand clothing. Knowing Burgess's reputation for having bizarre friendships, nobody thought anything of the incident until after his disappearance.

But then, anyone who had the slightest association with Burgess was cross-questioned closely, and his lunch companions of that day were no exception. They told the story of the letter, and, rather to their surprise, M.I.5 men then drove them to the area and asked them to point out the shop where the incident took place.

By sheer chance—for it had all happened many years before, and the couple had not been back since—they were able to identify it. The Intelligence officers nodded in satisfaction. "We have known for a long time that that was a 'post office' for Soviet agents," they said. By an odd coincidence, it was also the scene of a murder of some years before, when the murdered man was a physicist.

So here, then, is the first evidence that has come to light that Burgess actually used the facilities of the Soviet spy network, though for what purposes, of course, are unknown. His letter may have had an innocent explanation—perhaps he was writing to a sailor friend—or it may not.

That he was capable of treachery is undoubted. His

particular brand of amorality, combined with his intellectual conceit, enabled him to regard any information which came into his possession as his own personal property to do with as he wished. If, as in the Pfeiffer instance, he decided that a document should be suppressed it would present no insuperable moral hurdle. If, in his infinite wisdom, he decided that the information would be of value to whichever cause he was espousing at the time equally he would not hesitate to send it to them.

So much is abundantly clear. The real question is: did he set out on a deliberate course, ordered by a foreign power, to endeavour to obtain and supply information or in other ways use his position, friends and influence to achieve such ends?

Much has been made, in attempts to prove that Burgess was a deliberate and paid spy of the fact that he was often seen to have large sums of money on him, or that he left rolls of notes lying carelessly about his flat. But it would be extremely dangerous to draw conclusions either way from this evidence. It is more than likely, if Burgess was an active spy, that he was one from ideological rather than financial motives. But that certainly would not prevent him from accepting money for services rendered. And again the money might have been received from perfectly legitimate sources. Mrs. Rothschild, for example, may have preferred to pay for his services in cash, and it is certain that M.I.5 at this stage did.

Burgess, during the immediate pre-war years, did pass on information to M.I.5, particularly on Germany (which he in turn probably got from von Putlitz) and was paid for it. He was not in any way employed by M.I.5 but worked with them as a free-lance.

Mr. Selwyn Lloyd, explaining this rather extraordinary position in the House of Commons soon after Burgess and Maclean had departed, claimed that Burgess had only been recompensed for his efforts by expenses. All payments made by M.I.5 in these circumstances are, for obvious reasons, described as "expenses". Payments, too, are invariably made in cash. Any other form of payment might well tax even the ingenuity of a Burgess to explain, if hauled up before The Commissioner of Inland Revenue.

So the sums of money which Burgess left lying about are capable of a fascinating variety of explanations!

In December 1938, Guy Burgess decided to resign from the B.B.C. On the face of it, it was a strange decision. He was doing extremely well in his job. He was satisfying his urge to make friends and influence people and, to a degree, he had influence himself.

It has been suggested, by apologists for Burgess, that he resigned as a protest against Munich. This of course is nonsense. Burgess was not the sort of person to make dramatic and futile gestures, unless it was to achieve a definite purpose. In proportion to the importance of the issue, Burgess's action would have achieved just about as much as if he had been a liftman at the B.B.C.

The reason he resigned was quite different. A friend of his had just been appointed by the then head of the Secret Service to inaugurate a small and completely new branch of the Service and had been given a separate and very large budget on which to operate. The new department was to organise sabotage and propaganda, and became known as Section Nine. One of the first people the new chief of Section Nine invited to join the organisation was Guy Burgess.

Like so many aspects of the Burgess story, the alacrity with which he accepted this offer is capable of two interpretations. Without any other evidence the decision of a young man to give up a safe and secure job in which he was doing well for a temporary appointment with dubious prospects, but which offered the excitement and drama for which his soul yearned, would not be hard to accept as a probable one.

Equally it would be easy to claim that Guy Burgess's decision had the more sinister explanation that in the job he saw an opportunity to breach the Citadel.

The only comment that would seem irresistible is that the question of Burgess's motive in accepting the appointment should never have arisen. He should never have been offered it.

Be that as it may, the affairs of Section Nine did not prosper for long after the outbreak of war in the form in which it had been set up.

Burgess had persuaded his friend, the Chief of the Section, that he should go to Moscow to enlist the help of the Russians on a co-operative scheme for the supply of arms to the European underground movements. He got as far as Washington when he was recalled. He got back to find that he, his boss and most of the people he had brought into Section Nine had been fired.

Burgess returned to the B.B.C. His work was relatively unimportant and one wonders whether it ever occurred to him to take up the invitation offered to him by Churchill that afternoon in his garden at Westerham. The predictions that Churchill had made then had come true and one would have imagined the opportunity it offered Burgess was one that he would have seized with both hands.

The fact remains that he did not. Instead, by devious string-pulling, he managed to get himself transferred again from the safe haven offered by the B.B.C. (where he was now running an advice programme called "Can I Help You?") to the dubious status of temporary civil servant in the Foreign Office News Department.

It turned out for him, however, to be an inspired move. Whilst he was there he took the Foreign Office Competitive examination and succeeded in getting himself established as permanent staff.

Shortly after the war he was at his desk in the News Room, engaged on some routine task, when the telephone rang. At the other end was Hector McNeil, Labour Member of Parliament for Greenock, whom he had met in the old "Week in Westminster" days and with whom he had maintained contact ever since. McNeil had just been appointed to Cabinet rank in the Labour Government with the job of Minister of State at the Foreign Office and he wanted Burgess to be his Personal Assistant.

At last Guy Burgess, known to a wide circle of people

as a homosexual, alcoholic, suspected drug addict and Communist sympathiser, was very near indeed to the seat of power.

So far this account has made only passing reference to his drinking habits. It is, however, an important aspect in any appraisal of the man.

Burgess was a heavy drinker from his earliest Cambridge days. Derek Blaikie, on his return from their trip to Moscow, used to regale his Oxford colleagues with the story of losing Burgess and finding him, eventually, dead drunk in the Park of Rest and Culture.

It was only after he started to live in London, however, that his drinking assumed the proportions of a "compulsive" drinker. His favourite day-to-day drink was red wine, which he consumed in copious quantities; but it was when the whisky bottle came out that the trouble really began. Sir Harold Nicolson, who never disguised his admiration for Burgess—although he disapproved of his bitten and dirty fingernails!—remarks on the brilliance and colourfulness of his personality until he had had too many drinks. Then, he said, he became boring and incoherent.

Another friend who used to call in to see him from time to time in the Foreign Office remarks on the air of "good natured disorganisation and jollity" about the place. Like most of us, he was wont to regard the dignified, portentous atmosphere of the Foreign Office with considerable awe—until he visited Burgess in the Secretaries room which he shared with Minister of State Hector McNeil's other aide. It had, he said, "the

74

charm of being entirely untainted by industry, sobriety or decorum".

The fact that, on his return from luncheon, he was more often drunk than sober appears to have passed without comment even from McNeil, who remained a strong supporter and admirer of Burgess in spite of the severe trials to which his patience must have been put from time to time.

Another fascinating cameo of life as it was lived in that tea-cup-and-cigarette-strewn Secretaries Office is given by another of Burgess's friends, who called into the office to pick up a book which Burgess had promised to lend him.

As he was shown in the two aides were in the middle of a heated argument on the rival merits of two particularly seamy Soho drinking clubs. Suddenly the buzzer went. "What on earth can HE want?" HE, of course, being the harassed Minister.

"Perhaps you'd better go in, Guy."

"Oh no! He can't possibly want *me*. I've been in twice today. You go, Fred."

When, after a minute, the Minister had not rung again, they resumed their argument where they had left off, agreeing that it was really too bad of the Minister to have rung when obviously he did not want anything important.

The book in question was the Kinsey Report on *The Sexual Behaviour of the Human Male* which had not yet been published in this country but of which Burgess had had a special copy sent from America.

There had, he explained, been such a queue of Foreign Office officials who wanted to borrow it that he had had to lock it away in a safe place.

"I'll have to go and get it," he said. "You had better come with me."

I quote here, verbatim, the story as Burgess's friend told it to me.

"I followed him down the broad corridors of the Foreign Office," he recalled, "until we came to what was evidently a very important room indeed, and even Guy stood for a moment abashed on the threshold.

" 'It's all right,' he said, 'he's not in,' and pushing open the door, entered a vast room which seemed to be all red plush and rather heavy, brocaded curtains. A table ran the whole length of the room, and in the middle of it, with its back to the long windows, was a heavily and ornately carved chair.

" 'It's the Foreign Secretary's room,' explained Guy airily. 'I thought you'd like to see it. I love it.'

"In one corner of the room was an open safe, which had obviously long ceased to have any use for security purposes, as its doors stood open and the shelves within seemed to be filled with reference books. Guy fumbled among them for a moment then withdrew his hand holding the Kinsey Report.

" 'I keep it here,' he explained. 'I know no one would think of looking for it and, if Ernie found it, he would not know what it was—and even if he did he would not want to read it.' "

Amusing as these sidelights are, they paint an alarming,

if not perhaps typical, picture of life in one of our more august Ministries.

If Burgess was never reprimanded for his drinking habits at the Ministry in London, he was the subject of at least one critical inter-office memo which, like so much in his life, had all the overtones of high comedy. It read in its entire simplicity: "Mr. Burgess will, in future, refrain from munching garlic during office hours."

It sprang from a deplorable habit of using garlic, not as a flavouring but as a vegetable—a vegetable, moreover, which he carried around in his pockets, kept in the drawers of his desk and munched continuously to the distress and alarm of everyone around him.

Apart from lunch-time sessions, which usually took place at the Reform Club—where an extraordinarily large bumper of port is still known as a "double Burgess" —his drinking bouts, when they were not in his own or somebody else's flat, usually took place in Soho.

One of his favourite haunts was an afternoon and evening drinking club called the Mandrake, which had its being in a back street basement off Dean Street. This was in those days a very offbeat club, frequented by an extraordinary mixture of artists, writers, poets and hangers-on who seemed to have little to do all day but sit around drinking and playing endless games of chess. Burgess was a member of long standing, paying his guinea a year membership by Banker's Order—unlike Maclean who also used the club but never paid his subscription.

As the then proprietor Boris Watson says: "I often used to find Maclean there when I came down, either drinking by himself or with other friends who were not members. I chucked him out time and again, but he always used to try to get in again, usually when he was drunk."

They were never, however, so far as anyone can remember, seen there together.

Another favourite drinking club was the Gargoyle in Dean Street, which was then owned by the Hon. David Tennant. Tennant was married to actress Hermione Baddeley and between them they knew "everybody who was anybody" in London. For many years the Gargoyle was the late-night meeting place of café society and stage, political and literary names. For Burgess, the atmosphere of the Gargoyle was the very stuff of life itself, and he was a familiar figure there at the beginning of the war, until he left for Washington, en route for Moscow, on his short-lived job for Section Nine. The club has, incidentally, long since changed hands.

In spite of his, (to put it mildly) untidy private life there is some evidence, at this stage, that Guy Burgess might have made the grade as a diplomat. He had a strong ally in the person of Hector McNeil, who undoubtedly relied on him to a considerable extent as his personal *eminence grise*, and working in a private office rather than in a department, his personal eccentricities were not so apparent as they might have been. That he had access to highly secret information at this time is undoubted, though there has never been any evidence to suggest that any of this information was finding its way into the wrong hands.

Indeed McNeil, at this time, was bringing pressure to bear to get Burgess transferred from Branch B, to which he belonged, to the higher rating Branch A.

The Foreign Office would not agree to this on the grounds of his extremely limited experience. To counter this he asked to be moved to a political department, specifying that, if possible, he would like the Far Eastern Department, which dealt with China—a country in which he was deeply interested and on which he claimed to be something of an expert. It was, incidentally, also one of the few areas in which he found himself in agreement with British policy. Recognition of Communist China was, with his background, obviously a policy with which he could find little to quarrel. The failure of the Americans to do so was one of the principal reasons for his bitter and openly-voiced antagonism to them.

Of the few months he worked in the Far Eastern Section Burgess now says: "Anybody could be proud of the wisdom, the knowledge and the lack of prejudice of that department and the people in it." He also found it extremely agreeable that all his colleagues in this department, with one exception, were Old Etonians. His own behaviour, however, brought his appointment to an early close.

In the autumn of 1949 he took his leave abroad, touring in North Africa. With his insatiable appetite for involving himself in affairs which were not his concern, he made a point of calling on the various Secret Service representatives in places which he visited. And not only calling. He took the opportunity of impressing them with his own inside knowledge, making it at the same time unmistakably clear that his opinion of the British Secret Service in general and the representative to whom he was talking at the time in particular, was not of the highest.

Not unnaturally, when he returned to duty in the Far Eastern Department, it was to find that he was on the carpet. The various people he had visited had wasted no time in reporting what he had said.

So serious were the charges that a disciplinary Board was set up to investigate the matter. The charge was that he had been guilty of "serious indiscretion about intelligence matters".

He was severely reprimanded. At the same time he was told that his services would no longer be required in the Far Eastern Department, and that his prospects of promotion had been diminished.

Nevertheless Hector McNeil continued to take upon himself the task of forwarding his protégé's career. He considered that it was of vital importance for Burgess to serve in an Embassy abroad. Burgess agreed in principle, but his enthusiasm was tempered by the thought of leaving London, which he used to claim was the only capital in the world where life was supportable. He could think of no embassy where the life would appeal to him.

McNeil, however, was insistent and, in due course, the posting came through. In view of all that was, or ought to have been known of Burgess, the selection of the first Embassy where he was to serve abroad is almost unbelievable.

It was Washington.*

For Burgess it was the beginning of the end.

A week before Burgess arrived in Washington, Sir Robert Mackenzie, Regional Security Officer for north and central America, received an extraordinary report from London. While the contents have never been disclosed, they were of a nature to spread alarm and despondency in Sir Robert's office, where it was rightly considered that the security staff had enough to do without Whitehall adding to their burdens by sending out unreliable, unstable employees with a taste for drink and perhaps for other things as well. For the report was a summary of Burgess's background and career, and it said enough about his personal life to make them look to his arrival with foreboding.

At this point one must wonder what strange method, system or organisation allowed one department to send him to Washington and another to recommend that he should be watched because he was unfit for the job. If Burgess was sent on approval, as it were, it would seem to indicate a very hit-and-miss method of personnel selection.

The forebodings of the Embassy staff were quickly

* His posting to Washington was still as a member of the fourth grade of the junior branch, the rank with which he had joined in 1943. Surely at thirty-nine he was the oldest man ever to hold such a low rank in the history of the Foreign Service.

justified. Within a matter of weeks he was in trouble. The security officer, Squadron-Leader "Tommy" Thompson, carpeted him for what was officially described on the report as "carelessness with official papers". Burgess had left his office unlocked and a pile of secret papers scattered on his desk in his usual untidy fashion. They were not, in fact, Top Secret, or anything like it, but were confidential enough to be embarrassing in the wrong hands.

Burgess's reaction to this reprimand was one of disinterest. He wrote the required apology on the appropriate form as though he was explaining where he had lost his cheque-book. His attitude was considered to be more serious than the misdemeanour, and Thompson mentioned it to Sir Robert. By this time, as it happened, Whitehall had received a protest about Burgess's appointment from the Embassy, and a copy of the report about his first black mark was sent to Whitehall to back it up. There was no constructive reply to either, though the only reply which the Embassy would have considered constructive was one which would have meant his immediate return to U.K.

As we know from his friends, Burgess was more than unhappy in America, and this was reflected in his work and his drinking. His friends were, as usual, extraordinary in their variety. He spent some time regularly with Gladwyn Jebb (now Lord Gladwyn) in New York at the United Nations, and, in contrast, with a man in Washington who was a homosexual of the most unsavoury kind.

Tom Driberg, in his excellent study of Burgess—which he describes as "a sort of apologia"—puts his bad behaviour down to Burgess's sensitivity and emotional complexity, brought about, largely, by his reaction to British foreign policy and its subservience to the State Department.

There is no doubt that many diplomats felt the same way, but it is fortunate for the diplomatic service that they did not feel themselves to be above discipline and outside the compass of good manners. Driberg overlooks the character assessment of Burgess from friends from childhood: that he was spoilt and wilful, and that when very small he would scream and rage for hours until he got his own way. These childish characteristics were carried through into adult life, aided by a personality usually described as "dominating". So it is reasonable to assume that it was not entirely his distaste for the policy of Britain that led him to his American excesses, but also the fact that he was meeting opposition and people who actively disliked him—and Burgess had always liked to be liked.

His intellectual freedom was curtailed in America as it had never been in London. As a member of the Embassy staff he was subject to closer scrutiny than at home. No longer could he obtain a vicarious thrill by expounding outrageous social doctrines at cocktail parties—and by that I do not mean Communist doctrines, for Burgess had a political outlook of his own which did not fit any creed, and which he alternated at will and with great eloquence. He still shocked people, of course, and took a great delight in doing so, but in Washington and New York his views were naturally taken more seriously than in Mayfair, Soho and Chelsea, where so many of his listeners knew him as an amiable eccentric.

In America, cocktail parties usually included members of the F.B.I. or C.I.A., and they listened with misgivings to the man from the British Embassy. Whatever the rights and wrongs of their political views and attitudes, the Americans can be forgiven, as they listened to Burgess, for wondering: "Are these people hypocrites or fools or enemies?"

Burgess's reaction to this unfriendliness and hostility found expression in long, bitter memoranda to London in which he said in effect that no one at the Embassy was any use except, perhaps, the Ambassador and, by implication, himself. Our policies were wrong, he said, the execution of them was inept and the people who carried them out were hopeless. He was quite unsuited to his post, he admitted—but with the inference that he was unsuited because of his intellectual level, and that if he had committed any misdemeanours it was simply because the whole business was more than he could bear.

His "misdemeanours" however soon took a more sinister turn. One week-end while he was in Washington he stayed with a British diplomat. After lunch on Sunday he went for a stroll in the garden. His host was troubled. He had received a copy of a report from London which was the result of the M.I.5 enquiry into the leakage discovered in 1949. The stage it had now reached, the Report said, was a heartening one: from all the thousands of employees of the Foreign Office and its associate offices, four men had been listed as being principal suspects.

One of them—the principal one—was Donald Maclean.

Both the diplomat and Burgess knew Maclean, and the diplomat felt that some terrible mistake had been made. Knowing that Burgess had been friends with him at Cambridge he sought his opinion.

No one knows what went through Burgess's mind after this innocent disclosure. There is no evidence that he was at this period on terms of particular friendship with Maclean. Their ways had parted after Cambridge. But did the memory of the early relationship remain strong? Did he feel he must scheme to save Maclean? Did he simply feel that he must scheme to save anyone at odds with officialdom? One thing only is clear from studying his Washington career and that is that about this time he began putting up blacks in earnest. He was careless about official papers again, and was again reprimanded; he had a rather ostentatious row with Joseph Alsop, the famous American columnist; his drinking bouts became more dramatic and his friendships more bizarre; he was invited to lecture on Red China in the South and was stopped three times by traffic police on the way—all these incidents added up to just one certainty: that Guy Burgess's days in Washington were numbered, and he knew it.

The traffic offences were made all the more important because he had picked up an American homosexual with a police record, and the American State Department felt that this was hardly the way for a diplomat to behave. Burgess, typically, was full of bravado, complaining that he was driving at 100 mph when the police charge said he was only doing eighty; and again, that the Americans were only kicking up a fuss because the Governor of Virginia, where it all happened, was notoriously anti-British. (Back in London, he told a friend a completely contradictory story: that he had given a lift to a man, and that the man was actually driving when the speed limit was exceeded, but to save him from trouble Burgess pleaded diplomatic immunity to the traffic police.)

The complaints book was now full; the Ambassador sent for him and told him he would have to go, that he was a disgrace to the Foreign Service. Burgess took this calmly, even cheerfully. He spent his last few weeks in the Embassy library, reading.

The security officer, Thompson, who is now retired and licensee of a public-house in Wokingham, says that when he first met Burgess he wondered whether M.I.5 were playing some incredibly deep double game, so obviously unsuitable and unreliable was he.

It did not take long, however, says Thompson, to realise that unhappily there was nothing clever in his appointment at all, and his own objective then became the short-term one of how to get rid of Burgess before he had the opportunity of doing irreparable harm.

Before leaving the subject of Burgess in Washington, two names must be mentioned. The first is that of Harold (Kim) Philby, who much later was to be the centre of violent controversy.

Philby was the son of St. John Philby, the famous expert on Arab affairs, and had made a study of the subject himself. During the war he worked for M.I.5, and had made a considerable impression by his conscientious work. Whether M.I.5 knew at that time that he had been an equally conscientious Communist advocate of extreme left-wing views during his university life, and after, is not known and may be of little consequence. What is known is that Philby and Burgess were close friends, and had been at Cambridge together, so that when Burgess arrived in America it was natural that Philby should ask him to stay at his house, which he did.

This association gave rise to considerable speculation, after Burgess disappeared, that Philby had been associated with the disappearance. Mr. Harold Macmillan, in the House, defended him and said that no evidence had been found for presuming that he had been instrumental in warning Burgess or Maclean, and that while in government service he had carried out his duties ably and well. Nevertheless, the effect of the accusation (originally by Col. Marcus Lipton and Lord Elton) was sufficient to have serious repercussions on Philby's life in the Foreign Office. He is now the correspondent for *The Observer* in Beirut.

Let us look at the Parliamentary report of *The Times* on the White Paper debate which deals with Philby:

"Mr. Daines (East Ham, North, Lab.) said that Lieut-Col. Lipton had made a charge against Mr. Philby in a question. He owed it to the House to give the sources of the information on which that charge was based.

"Lieut-Col. Lipton, after some other interruptions, said the statement he had made concerning Mr. Philby on October 25 was quite a serious one, and he was convinced that in making it he was serving the public by forcing the government, and in particular the Foreign Secretary, to provide much more information than had been provided hitherto.

"Mr. Nutting, Minister of State for Foreign Affairs (Melton, C)—Will the hon. member be good enough to forward to the Foreign Secretary the evidence on which he is basing his charges against Mr. Philby?

"Lieut-Col. Lipton—No. (laughter). I am prepared to forward that information to a judicial member of the Privy Council who, it has been suggested, should carry out an investigation into the secret service. When the verbal niceties of the Foreign Secretary's speech have been examined it will be found that I am justified in not making a withdrawal at the present time."

However, Lipton did make a withdrawal and an apology later.

Incidentally, the immediate consequences of his original allegation were dramatic. He was approached afterwards and asked to attend an informal meeting of the Foreign Office security men and M.I.5. This in itself did not surprise him but the information that they gave him at the meeting did. "As a result I was glad to apologise to

Philby," he says now. "But I must say that I was more concerned about our security service when I came out than when I went in." In the briefing that he had been given there was material for a dozen embarrassing Questions—but as it had been given to him in confidence there was nothing he could do.

The second name that crops up is that of Anthony Eden.

Out of all the turmoil, mental agony and unhappiness which his short stay in Washington represented to Guy Burgess there is only one memory which he treasured.

Shortly after his arrival Anthony Eden paid a visit to Washington. Eden was not then Foreign Secretary so the visit was an unofficial one. On the other hand the next election was looming on the horizon and it was quite likely that he would again be in office in the near future. Guy Burgess was the Embassy official deputed to look after Eden.

After he left he wrote a letter to Burgess in which he expressed his gratitude.

> *Government House,*
> *8th November, 1950*
> *Ottawa*

My dear Burgess,

Thank you so much for all your kindness. I was so well looked after that I am still in robust health, after quite a stormy flight to New York and many engagements since! Truly I enjoyed every moment of my stay in Washington, and you will know how much you helped to make this possible. Renewed greetings and gratitude,

Yours sincerely,

Anthony Eden

P.S. Incidentally that very friendly footman hadn't after all searched those evening trousers very well for I found in them those dollars and this key—so sorry! A.E.

This letter is now one of his most valued possessions and he still shows it to his friends in Moscow.

Describing this Washington period for me, a close friend of Burgess who must remain anonymous has written: "Guy himself had no illusions about his suitability for the post, and if he could possibly have managed to remain in London he would have. We discussed all this one evening shortly before he left, and he did not conceal his gloom at the prospect before him. He spoke again of resigning from the Foreign Office, and I could not really understand why he did not, because I could not see that there was any future in it for him; but then one could not really see that there was any future for him in anything. All the more because, in recent months—for the first time since I knew him—he had become short of money.

"It was one of the oddest aspects of his character that, despite all his irresponsibility, his complete lack of self-control in pursuing anything he wanted, his gift for provoking personal disasters, there were some faults from which he was completely free. He never missed an

BURGESS, THE BACKGROUND

appointment, he was never late, and until just before he
left for Washington, he never ran into debt.

"But now he borrowed money from a friend of mine,
and I later learned he had borrowed money from a friend
of his. I was surprised, because I could not see any change
in his circumstances to account for this, and it marked so
great a change from a pattern of behaviour that had per-
sisted for so long that I could not help being puzzled by
it."

The point about money is not without interest. As a
junior member of the Foreign Office, even when he was
doing an important job as private secretary to the
Minister, his salary fell very far short of a thousand a year.
In fact when he was sent to Washington his basic salary
was only £700. On top of this he had a private income in
the region of £500. It is doubtful if, during the whole
time he was in London, he earned much over £2,000,
including benefits from Mrs. Rothschild and odd amounts
picked up from M.I.5 and other sources. This would
certainly not be enough to maintain life on the scale at
which he lived.

As I have remarked before, however, it would be
dangerous to draw any obvious or sinister conclusions
on a subject which must be largely conjectural.

5

The Macleans

As we have seen on the face of it the tall, slim, almost-good-looking undergraduate Donald Maclean had had little in common with Guy Burgess.

Yet, beneath the surface, it was different. They both had active and agile minds, they were both politically aware and they were both immensely ambitious.

There is no doubt that, apart from the sexual claims which Burgess makes, Maclean found Burgess intellectually stimulating and was influenced by Burgess into joining the Communist Party.

Listening to Burgess's brilliant eloquence, the ideas and attitudes of his father must have seemed very out-of-date and inadequate; Liberalism was like a Noah donning a macintosh to cope with the Flood.

Side by side with studying languages, Maclean began to analyse Marxism. There was no shortage of books to be borrowed on the subject, and no lack of friends to discuss them. Burgess was the centre of a brilliant coterie and from them Maclean found most of the answers to his questions. Soon he was another Burgess "convert" to communism and, as with most things in his life, once he had made a decision, he stuck to it.

His Foreign Office application was as much a matter of necessity as inclination; there was little else offering

92

itself to him, and it was a safe if financially unrewarding start in life in a very insecure world for postgraduates. The honours degree (German and French) helped him to pass the entrance examination with ease, though without outstanding brilliance.

His first three years were spent behind a desk in Whitehall. He made sufficient impression to be posted to Paris in 1938 as Third Secretary to the Embassy. This promotion pleased him immensely; it was good for his ego and his income. The social life of Paris, too, appealed to a latent Bohemian streak in his nature which financial considerations and family upbringing had so far held in check.

In the heady atmosphere of pre-war Paris the young personable diplomat started to grow up fast.

In a left-bank bistro, the Café de Flore, one night, there was a new face among his friends: a pretty, pert American girl studying French literature and art appreciation at the Sorbonne. Her name was Melinda Marling. They were introduced by two people who knew both of them: a young Englishman, Mark Culme-Seymour, and an American writer, Robert McAlmon.

Melinda was gay, exciting and intelligent. She was also moderately left-wing, though, like Maclean, there was nothing in her background to make her so. Her family were middle-class Americans; rich and getting richer. Her parents had separated in 1928, and soon afterwards Mrs. Marling took her three daughters, Harriet, Catherine and Melinda, to Switzerland for a European finishing-school education. Mother returned to America to finalise a divorce and to marry Hal Dunbar, another wealthy businessman. They brought the children back from Lausanne and set up home in New York, sending Melinda to the Spence School, an exclusive establishment for top-drawer young ladies. She left after three years, bored and restless, to take a secretarial course (dropped half-way through) and a job at Macy's (abandoned after a few months).

But this vapid, spoilt life, with indulgent parents providing everything she wanted, could not go on. Underneath, she was dissatisfied but undecided what to do. She knew she was wasting important years, so almost on impulse took a ticket to Paris. She had friends there from her Swiss schooldays, and they quickly introduced her to the Left Bank life. In those days it was an exciting one, with Picasso and Cocteau dominating the scene.

From their meeting in the Café de Flore, however, Melinda Marling and Donald Maclean were inseparable; he eclipsed all her other friends. He was a suave, competent, worldly diplomat, equally at home with the artistic chatter of a Paris bistro as he was in the cool, calm formal elegance of an embassy reception. He was an intellectual, his knowledge of art and literature was advanced, his arguments were persuasive and learned, he was an expert on politics and economics; international affairs were his living.

Melinda could not meet him at any point on the intellectual plane, but the breadth of his learning fascinated her, stimulated her and certainly impressed her. With his good looks and titled background, he was the embodiment of most middle-class American girls' dreams.

She was devoted to him, was infatuated by him perhaps, but she held back from thoughts of marrying him. Time strengthened their friendship, yet had no effect on her matrimonial views. He was a good friend, someone to show off to her friends. No more than that.

There was a reason for this; a flaw in Donald—his drinking. Even in those early days the pattern of what was to be his life was beginning to show. The periodical drinking bouts which, once started upon, did not end until he collapsed in helpless oblivion. The lapses into homosexuality, the unreasoning furies, the bouts of violence which marked the various stages of his drunkenness were already traits which made his friends apprehensive and worried for his future.

Melinda knew about them and was worried too. It was the only thing that made her hesitate; to continue to think of Donald as a good friend and not as a prospective husband.

There seemed to be some force inside him which would suddenly take control and change the considerate, affectionate, intelligent man she admired and loved into a brutal, loutish stranger.

Even before she married him, she tried to make him see reason. "If you do feel an urge to have a drinking orgy," she wrote to him, "why don't you have it at home —at least you will be able to get safely to bed."

It was an appeal she was to repeat many times in the next few years.

Maclean remained *en poste* in Paris during the period

of the phoney war. Then Hitler launched his blitzkrieg, the Allied armies were pushed back from the Maginot Line in disorganised retreat and soon the relentless German forces, at the peak of their power, were nearing Paris.

Maclean chose that moment of turmoil and apprehension to ask Melinda to marry him. At first she refused. Maclean urged her to reconsider. Again she refused.

Maclean accepted her decision and told her he would drive her to Bordeaux and see her safely on a boat bound for her neutral homeland. And then Melinda changed her mind as she watched the hurried, frenzied evacuation of Paris begin. They ploughed through the formidable formalities and were married on June 10 with the sound of gunfire just audible in the far distance. Maclean— calm, confident, sure; Melinda—anxious, nervous, still doubtful.

Now to get away from the Nazi war machine. They had a car and joined the mass migration from Paris. But they had not counted on roads choked with evacuees and they only reached Chartres on the first day and had to spend their first night as man and wife in a field. Then on to Bordeaux and on the 13th day of their marriage they sailed from France in a British destroyer, transferred to a collier after three hours at sea, and arrived in Britain at the end of a ten-day zigzag voyage dodging dive bombers and U-boats.

Maclean stayed on in war-time London for the next four years. Melinda, expecting their first baby in 1941, sailed to America for the birth, but the child was still-born and she flew sadly back to be with her husband despite the Nazi bombs then tearing London apart.

They were bombed out of two flats and once they were nearly killed in an air raid. But Melinda stuck it out, spending her days working in The Times Book Shop. When the air raid sirens wailed, she refused to take cover in a shelter. She tried it once and hated it. "I'd rather die in bed than face it again," she said.

But worse than the bombs, for Melinda, were the constant rows they were having, sparked off by Donald's drinking and fanned by her own fiery temper.

The fears which she had so impetuously brushed aside in those last unreal days before the fall of Paris were being realised. Although they still had times of almost idyllic happiness they were fewer and further between.

Then, for Melinda, hope flared again. In April 1944 Donald was appointed to Washington. For him the job at the Embassy as First Secretary was promotion. For her it meant a return to her homeland, her mother, her sisters and the possibility of a saner, less worrying way of life.

However, it was not to be.

Donald's attitude towards her when they first reached America was strange. She was pregnant and he left her with her mother while he went to Washington. He shared an apartment with a colleague and claimed that he could not find suitable accommodation for his wife to join him. Yet the Embassy would have found them a place to live if he had asked them to do so; even if prices were high he could have had his housing allowance stepped up. He rarely sent her money, forcing her to live off her wealthy mother, although he knew she disliked being put in that position.

In the autumn of 1944 their first child, Donald Fergus, was born by a Caesarian operation and Maclean's attitude changed. He was thrilled with the baby. He went back to Washington, found an apartment, and brought his wife and baby son to live with him. They were together for Christmas.

Though his personal life was unsettled, his professional career was gratifyingly stable. The promise of his earlier years was becoming reality and he was promoted again, to acting Counsellor and Head of Chancery. He seemed certain, at the war's end, to enjoy a long and distinguished life in the Foreign Service.

His new position in the Embassy was that of chief administrative officer. He saw most of the documents received and despatched, and at this time they included a vast amount of correspondence and memoranda of the highest scientific and political importance. British and American scientists had worked in close co-operation on the atomic bomb that blasted Japan out of the war, and in the years that followed, the secrets of that bomb were the subject of delicate diplomatic negotiation between Britain and America, the Soviet agents were making desperate efforts to discover not only the scientific processes but the political policies of the Western atomic powers.

Maclean was thus in a unique position to help them,

as, many years later, M.I.5 came to suspect that he had done. His private life about this time underwent yet another change, and if, as some of his friends believe today, this was the period when he first worked actively for Russia, this change may have had considerable bearing on it. Certainly, he became violently anti-American and began to drink more heavily than ever.

It was a time when Britain and America had done a smart about-turn on Russia. From the war-time "gallant Soviet allies" they had become the peace-time "menace to the civilised world". Maclean, too, was in a country that regarded Communism as a dirty word. For a man who had studied Russia so closely in the early thirties and who had obviously been so much in sympathy with Communism, Western policy was certain to produce bitter reaction in his mind.

Maclean's heavy drinking, his sexual tendencies and his sour outlook on America made him vulnerable to a skilled Soviet agent, although it is likely that he had never anyway lost touch with the Party. Undoubtedly, however, his disagreement with American policy could have done much, at this time, to inflame him to an active rather than a passive role.

What had he to offer to a Soviet agent? A great deal, although after his disappearance the Foreign Office was at great pains to undervalue his knowledge and, indeed, there were denials that he was in possession of atomic secrets. This was true—if by atomic secrets it was meant the algebraic formulae that Nunn May or Fuchs or Pontecorvo took with them. Maclean's knowledge was of the political background, and this was every bit as important—if not more so, for by this time the Russians were already far advanced in the scientific field.

On the other hand he knew the general heads of agreement between Great Britain, Canada and the U.S.; he knew the points of divergence; he knew the reasons for co-operation in some fields and the lack of it in others. He knew how many atomic bombs we had, the amounts of uranium 235 available and the manufacturing potential with existing resources and materials.

"My God," exclaimed Dean Acheson when first told the news of Maclean's defection, "he knew everything!"

This statement was hastily modified, but the reaction was significant.

It also contrasts strangely with the statement made by Herbert Morrison in the House of Commons shortly after the disappearance. Asked specifically whether Maclean had in his possession any atomic secrets he categorically denied that he had.

Dean Acheson was the more correct.

One of the positions of extreme responsibility which Maclean held extramurally to his Embassy duties, was Secretary to the Combined Committee on Atomic Development, with a pass which admitted him to the Atomic Energy Commission offices at any time of the day or night.

Quite apart from this he had studiously devoted himself to the study of the political aspects of atomic energy and was regarded in the Foreign Office as their expert on this subject, as an incident which I will describe later shows.

For Melinda, these four years in America were miserable years. Maclean neglected her, vented his anger against America on her, and she had to continue to suffer from his excessive drinking. But, as in the Blitz on Britain, she bore her troubles bravely.

Their second child was born in July, 1946. She went to New York again for the birth and again it was a son, Donald Marling.

The child was two in 1948 when Maclean was appointed Head of Chancery in Cairo and the family sailed to England in September for home leave before Maclean took up his new post.

They were both excited at the prospects before them. Maclean was happy to leave the America he loathed, and Melinda was eagerly looking forward to a new life. With characteristic resilience the disappointment of her American hopes was already forgotten. But the cracks in the Maclean façade, first visible in America, were now beyond repair; in Cairo, the façade crumbled completely.

Their home in the Egyptian capital was three-storied, big and spacious, the garden filled with luxurious flowers and plants, tall trees providing welcome shade from the sun. It was a house built for senior British officials, furnished and maintained by the government. The Macleans had four servants, gardeners and an English governess for the children. Cairo could have been idyllic for them.

Melinda was happy enough at the outset. Maclean seemed to have settled down in his new post and to be enjoying his work. She quickly made many friends on the eternal cocktail party round and she was asked to arrange at short notice a party for the Duke of Edinburgh. He was visiting Cairo, staying at the British Embassy, and the party was planned to relieve the monotony of the stiff and starchy official programme. It was held at the Maclean home in Gezireh and the guests were drawn from Cairo's younger element. Fourteen sat down to dinner with the Duke; other guests came after the meal. It was a party at which they played such games as "Murder" and it proved riotously successful. It was a triumph for the once-shy girl from Chicago.

But after about six months, Maclean began to dislike Egypt. He contrasted the affluence and the social whirl of the few with the miserable poverty of the many. He despised the arrogance and ostentation so often to be seen. His communist soul revolted.

He objected, too, to British policy in the Canal Zone; he considered the wait-and-see attitude to be stupid; he thought Britain should urge the Egyptian government to reform the social structure of the country and attempt to ease the misery of the masses.

So he began to drink again. Only this time his drinking bouts were much more serious than they had been in Washington. They led to troubles in the home and incidents outside which could not be hushed up. People began to talk.

One of the first incidents found him in a drunken

stupor on a park bench without his shoes. But that could be laughed off as an isolated incident, the result of a gruelling stint at the Embassy.

The next was far more serious. It happened when Melinda's sister, Harriet, came to stay with them. One day Melinda gathered a party of eight and hired a felucca to sail the fifteen miles to Helouan to visit friends who had a house on the banks of the Nile. There was plenty to drink on the wide-sailed boat, though little to eat, for they expected to have dinner when they arrived. But the wind dropped and the boat was almost becalmed; the trip took eight hours instead of the two that would have been the normal journey time.

Maclean found consolation in the bottles on board. When they arrived, he was paralytically drunk.

Before the party reached Helouan, they had an example of what to expect from him. He picked a quarrel with Melinda, seized her round the neck and began to squeeze. The rest of the party dragged him away from her: she might have been strangled if they had not been close at hand.

It was about 2 a.m. when the boat was drawing into the bank at their destination and the party was far from quiet. An alarmed river guard challenged them as they stepped ashore and the drunken Maclean immediately attacked him. He pulled the guard's loaded rifle from his hands, threatening to smash his skull. One member of their party tried to stop Maclean and to get the gun from him. Maclean refused to hand over the rifle, the two began struggling on the river bank, then slipped and both fell on to a wooden jetty. Maclean landed on top, and the other man had a leg broken in the fall.

The friends they had gone to visit would not let them in the house after hearing their condition and presumably did not believe the story of their plight. Eventually, they managed to hire a car to take them—and the man with the broken leg—back to Cairo. They arrived there just before Maclean was due to report for duty at the Embassy, in the morning.

Soon afterwards, Maclean invited a journalist friend to stay with them and the two spent much of their spare time drinking. That led to the worst episode of Maclean's Cairo days. This was when Harriet was still with the Macleans. The journalist made up a foursome and they all set off one evening to a cocktail party. Melinda, who was not well, left early, the journalist went to an engagement of his own, leaving Maclean and Harriet to go to another party.

By midnight, Maclean was almost drunk and Harriet, now bored with it all, decided to leave. Maclean stayed on drinking. About 2 a.m., he returned home, picked up his journalist friend, and together they went out on the town. Many more drinks and a few night clubs later, with dawn just breaking, they thought it would be a good idea to call on an Embassy friend. He let them into his flat, saw their condition, gave them a bottle of whisky in response to their demands for drink, and went back to bed. Later, when he left for the Embassy, they were still there, very drunk.

During the day, when the effects of the liquor began

to wear off, they remembered that a girl employed as a librarian in the American Embassy had a flat in the same building. They set out to find it and get more to drink.

A cleaner was in the flat when they finally found it. They pushed past her and helped themselves to all the drink they could find. Then they decided to tear the flat apart. They smashed a table, broke the bath by dropping a heavy slab of marble in it, chopped up some of the furniture and pushed as much of the girl's clothing as they could find down the lavatory. Satisfied, they returned to the other flat in the building and went to sleep.

Melinda found them there that night. She and Harriet dragged the pair of them out to a car and drove them home. That was the end for Melinda. She decided that Maclean could not go on with his dangerous drunken orgies; that drastic action had to be taken to bring him to his senses. Next morning, she had a long talk with Maclean and then went to see the Ambassador.

She explained that Maclean was ill, suffering from a nervous breakdown, and that it was vital for him to return to London for treatment by his own doctor. By now, Maclean's personal standing at the Embassy was suffering from the tales being spread about his drinking bouts and the Ambassador readily agreed to Melinda's suggestion.

No time was wasted. Two days after the flat-smashing episode Melinda drove him out to Farouk Field and saw him off on a London-bound plane. That was Friday, May 11, 1950, and his spell in Cairo had lasted a mere eighteen months.

The following day, from his mother's Kensington home, he wrote to Melinda:

"I am so grateful to you, my sweet, for taking all you have had to put up with without hating me. I am still rather lost, but cling to the idea that you do want me to be cured and come back. I am weary of making promises of being a better husband since past ones have all been broken; but perhaps if some technician will strengthen my gasket and enlarge my heart I could make a promise which would stick. Anyhow, you have been very sweet to me and I will try to give you something in return. I was overwhelmed with sadness at leaving the boys; I suppose it affects one particularly because they expect one to be there and have no means of understanding why one goes away; it is, however, I suppose bathetic rather than pathetic so long as they are happy; I know you will keep them so. I hate having left you with all the responsibility for the house, family, car, servants, and long to hear that you are managing all right."

He ended: "I think very much of you, my darling, miss you badly and love you. Don't feel sad about me as I will come back a better person and we can be happy together again I am sure."

The Foreign Office sent Maclean to their consultant psychiatrist who recommended that he should go to a clinic for an unspecified period. But Maclean refused, explaining in a letter to his wife: "I do not feel that I can face going into a clinic. Fear plays a leading part in my resistance but I also much doubt that there is any point in it." Instead, he went to a woman psychiatrist who had been recommended to him. Oddly enough, the Foreign Office agreed and gave him six months' sick leave.

His drinking went on—some of his friends said they rarely saw him sober during his sick leave—but he went regularly to his own psychiatrist. Their talks were concerned with his drinking and the psychiatrist is said to have told him that this was caused by a guilt complex, the result of his treatment of Melinda. He claimed he could not bear the sight of her; that this was why he drank; that it turned him to homosexuality. But how does this compare with his letter to her on his arrival in London from Cairo . . . "I think very much of you, my darling, miss you badly and love you . . ."

Meanwhile, Melinda in Cairo was left in a state of worried suspense. She had to cope with a pile of bills Maclean had left behind, a large house to run, the rumours surrounding Maclean's sudden flight to London, and the doubts concerning her husband's future. Her position was made worse when an Egyptian paper heard of Maclean's final drunken exploit in Cairo and published an account of it with a few trimmings added for good measure. It was good ammunition for the anti-British campaign and other Egyptian papers published the story. Whatever their private thoughts, her friends remained loyal to her and the Embassy officials were reassuring.

In times of trouble, too, Melinda could always rely on her mother. Three weeks after Maclean left her in

Cairo, Mrs. Dunbar arrived and took charge. She paid the bills, dealt with the servants who had become idle and a little cheeky, decided that they should leave Egypt and spend the summer in Spain, and supervised the packing for the journey. That all took three weeks and then Melinda and her mother sailed away to Spain with the two children.

Maclean could easily have joined them in Spain but he made no such suggestion. He stayed on in London and kept in touch by rather irregular letters. After they had been apart for about four months, though, Melinda received from him a letter written when he was in a state of acute melancholia. He said he could not see why she should ever return to him, he doubted if he would ever be a good husband or a good father, and that Melinda and the children would be better off without him after the way he had behaved. Melinda immediately cut short the Spanish holiday, travelled as far as Paris with her mother and the children, and went on alone to London and her husband.

She found the melancholy mood was persisting. They discussed the outlook for their future life together and Maclean expressed doubts about their ability to be happy. She talked, too, with the psychiatrist who was treating him and with some of his relatives and friends. She realised how much they had changed: how she had become more of an extrovert and enjoyed mixing with bright, simple people; that Maclean would have none of this and preferred deep, intense people and topics. But she was swayed by those who told her how much he was dependent on her; that he would be a lost soul in a wilderness of alcoholic unreality without her steadying hand.

Finally, they decided to try again. Melinda collected the children from Paris and wrote to her sister, Harriet:

> "Donald is still pretty confused and vague about himself and his desires, but I think when he gets settled he will find a new security and peace. I hope so. He hasn't had any drinking bouts since I have been back, but I can see that the root of the trouble is still not cleared away."

Maclean told his superiors at the Foreign Office that he had no wish to go abroad again for some time and would like to stay in London. This was agreed and he was appointed head of the American Department. In this position, the diplomatic social round made few demands on him and the temptation to drink was therefore reduced to a minimum. He arranged to start work again on November 1, 1950.

Their plan was to live well away from London. Maclean would travel to and from the office by train each day and the journey would discourage him from drinking in London when his working day was over. They began looking for a house in Kent and made their base at an hotel in Sevenoaks. It took them about two months to find what they wanted—a big, isolated house called Beaconshaw in the village of Tatsfield, not far from Biggin Hill.

Cooking, cleaning and the routine jobs in a house

were new to Melinda—she had been accustomed to servants all her life and at Beaconshaw she had only one part-time help. She had, too, to tackle the vast amount of work involved in setting up a new home—the curtain-making, the carpet-fitting and the decorating. Outside, a large, badly-neglected garden cried out for attention. The two children were frequently in ill-health and coupled with everything else she found she was pregnant again. She had little time to ponder on her marital problems.

Maclean began in fine style. On most nights he caught the early train to Oxted and drove the four miles from the station to Tatsfield, arriving in time for an evening meal. Melinda was delighted and was looking forward to a new era of domestic tranquillity and stability. But as winter gave way to spring, Maclean gave way to temptation. Occasionally, at first, he missed the early train. The "misses" became more frequent. Then he began to miss all the trains and to stay in London for the night. Once he was mixed up in a scene at a London dance club to which the police were called. On several occasions Melinda heard nothing from him for two or three days.

By May, his drinking had reached Cairo proportions. Frequently, he arrived at the Foreign Office, reached into a desk drawer for a bottle of whisky and took a large drink before he could begin his work. And it was nothing strange for him to arrive at cocktail parties completely drunk.

His anti-American diatribes were as fervent as ever. One night, after a dinner-party in Chelsea, he asked a friend, a well-known portrait painter: "What would you say if I told you I was working for Uncle Joe?"

The painter replied that he might regard it as a joke, or he might not. He would not know what to think.

"Well, anyway," said Maclean, "I am."

There was an embarrassed silence for a moment, the painter wondering how drunk Maclean was, Maclean staring fixedly at the carpet. The remark was not pursued, but Maclean soon launched into a bitter criticism of current American foreign policy which became almost hysterical. The painter was bored; he had heard it all before many times, and when Maclean got into this state he was unmanageable and unstoppable. The remark about "working for Uncle Joe" was a new one but not, he thought, to be taken seriously. The painter can hardly be blamed for not acting upon it, though M.I.5 did not take this view later.

Another incident of the same sort occurred one night, or rather in the early hours of the morning, in the Gargoyle Club, which Maclean, like Burgess, used to frequent when in London—and particularly when he was in the middle of a drinking bout and had missed the last train home.

A close friend of Guy Burgess, who knew Maclean but had not seen him since his Cambridge days over fifteen years before, was sitting with a party in a corner two tables away from one occupied by Maclean, who was now very drunk, staring with fixed intensity in his direction. He took no notice and indeed at first did not even remember who he was.

Suddenly Maclean got up from his table and lurched over to where he was sitting and said in a slurred but extremely belligerent voice: "I know all about you, Mister Bloody . . . . . You used to be one of us, but you ratted." For a moment it looked as if he were going to pick a fight. Then suddenly his legs crumpled under him and he was brought abruptly to his knees. There he stayed, his hands gripping the edge of the table and his large white face peering over the top of it; from which undignified position he proceeded to direct a stream of incoherent abuse. After a few moments of this he managed to regain his feet and stumbled unsteadily back to his table.

The man who was the object of this extraordinary scene had in fact been extremely left-wing politically in his youth. Although he had never been a member of the Communist Party, the only explanation he could put on Maclean's words was that Maclean had thought he had been and had "ratted".

A few weeks before he disappeared, Harriet came to stay with the Macleans and found Donald strained and worried. He complained of the tedium of his daily journey to the office and said that he longed to finish with it. He talked to her about communism in the same terms as to Melinda and others—though, for her, this subject was one she had not heard from him before.

No one, not even his closest friends, has any idea when

Maclean first discussed the possibility of going to Moscow with Melinda, but it is nonsense to suggest, as some authorities have, that he did not. His wife was by now just as ardently anti-American, politically, as her husband, and by her repetitive arguments, just as boring. This is not to say, however, that a move was being planned; far from it. But Maclean must have noticed that secret papers, which had been crossing his desk as a matter of routine, were not appearing any more. He knew of conferences which had taken place and which he would have attended normally, but which he had not because he was not invited. He suspected even that he was being followed. All this no doubt accounted for the "strain" which Harriet noted.

Would he have failed to discuss this with his wife? Perhaps. But his friends think that he certainly did, and those who know Melinda believe that she might even have suggested Moscow as a way out.

Burgess arrived back in London from Washington on May 7, 1951. Maclean had already been back from Cairo for a year.

It was the first time that the two men had been in the same country since Burgess had joined the Foreign Office. Now Burgess was suspended and, as a result of the report he had earned in Washington, his resignation had been asked for.

When he had been in Washington he had met Michael Berry, a friend from Eton days, and suggested that if he resigned from the Foreign Office he might look for a job in Fleet Street. Berry had seemed quite keen on the idea that he should come and work for him on the *Daily Telegraph*.

For Burgess it was a time to take stock and to decide where he was going to from there.

For Maclean the position was equally fluid, and a trifle more dangerous than the one in which Burgess found himself.

In April the two-year-long security investigations to locate the leak of information from inside the Foreign Office had narrowed the possibilities down to two men.

Now, at the beginning of May, there was only one name on the list. It was that of Donald Maclean.

One of the handful of people who knew of this investigation and of Maclean's danger was of course Guy Burgess. It had inadvertently been disclosed to him during the walk on the lawn back in Washington.

So the first person he must contact on his return to England was Maclean. But he could not ring the Foreign Office direct. The telephone might be tapped and he might be compromised enough already without sticking his head into such an obvious noose. Instead, he called Lady Maclean, Donald's mother, and asked her for her son's private address.

This caution indicates very clearly Burgess's state of mind at the time. He had, after all, a perfectly good and innocent reason for calling Maclean without having to resort to this roundabout method of communication. He had brought back with him from America a paper he had written on relations with China. He wanted to discuss it with someone before submitting it. What more natural person than his old friend who happened to be head of the American Section?

Instead, he contacted Maclean at Tatsfield and they arranged to meet for lunch, not, as one might expect, at either Maclean's club, the Travellers, or Burgess's, the Reform. Instead they lunched at the R.A.C., quite the most unlikely club for two diplomats to meet at—which was, of course, why they chose it. It would never do for the suspected spy and the disgraced official to be seen together by their colleagues.

Over lunch they talked, not about Burgess's paper on China, but about the information he had picked up in Washington. It was confirmation of something Maclean already suspected.

Maclean told Burgess that he knew he was being followed. "They even bumped into the back of my cab when I stopped suddenly yesterday. I got a good look at them," he said.

They met twice again after that and it was agreed that something would have to be done. But what? Burgess, as always, was full of confidence. It was a situation in which he revelled. The cloaks were on and the daggers were out. He would see that matters were put right for his old friend and Communist Party protégé of those gay Cambridge days. After all, this was obviously an M.I.5 operation, and in this sphere Burgess had powerful friends.

Little has come to light about Burgess's relations with M.I.5. Why? It is at least as important in trying to assess the degree of his guilt as the mass of evidence on his private habits to which so much publicity has been given.

As I have already remarked, anything to do with the Secret Service had an irresistible attraction for Burgess. In fact, any mention of a secret and he was like a small boy with a locked box that rattles. He would never be satisfied until he had seen inside.

And Burgess *had* seen the inside of the British Secret Service box. Not only had he done free-lance work for them before the war, but he had been employed by them for a spell of over a year in the critical days of the beginning of the war.

And he had many very close friends in high places— particularly in M.I.5.

There had even been a time, when he was at the Foreign Office after the war, when he had shared a flat with a man who was not only a distinguished art critic but was an important official of M.I.5.

These two had been on the terms of closest friendship since Trinity College days and knew each other's way of living as well as any two men could.

Then there was the regular Monday night at the Chelsea Palace in the King's Road.

Burgess adored music hall and particularly he adored the Chelsea Palace, now closed.

Everything that Burgess liked, his friends were required to like too, and each week, when the show changed, it was the time-honoured custom for Burgess to go along with a party. The party was always the same;

just four. One was a woman friend of long standing and intimacy. One worked for M.I.5. The other for M.I.6.

We get perhaps the closest look at Burgess's extraordinarily mixed bag of intimates at a private party he gave at his flat in Bond Street, which he shared with Jack Hewit, the telephone boy who so long ago had listened in to Henlein's conversations, just before leaving for his ill-fated adventures in Washington. A guest who was present has given me this description:

"There was Hector McNeil, then Secretary for Scotland; Mr. Kenneth Younger, McNeil's successor at the Foreign Office, and Burgess's current boss; Putlitz the spy; Professor (now Sir) Anthony Blunt; two young men who had obviously been picked up off the streets either that very evening or not long before; a couple of strange women, two men from M.I.5 and one from M.I.6, and a distinguished writer."

The party got off to a brisk start with a large quantity of mixed drinks. One of the young men then hit a guest with a bottle and, later on, his companion went back to the distinguished writer's flat and after staying an hour left with his host's wallet. A detailed description of the remainder of the party would be the same as that of any Bohemian Bacchanalian shindig; the important fact is that the guest-list included three security men, one of whom, at least, was a homosexual. Another source, incidentally, says that this man was an active supporter of the Comintern before the war, but renounced his association with the signing of the Nazi-Soviet pact in 1939.

While Burgess was busily finding out the extent of the suspicion attached to his friend, Maclean was in a confident, relaxed mood, doubtless engendered by Burgess's reassurances.

For instance, at one of his weekly lunches with Mark Culme-Seymour at the Garrick public-house, off Trafalgar Square, Maclean discussed at length the domestic problems that another child would bring. Melinda's confinement was barely a month off, and he was anxious, as might be expected. He was also talking of obtaining a transfer in the Foreign Office, and went into detail. "It could all have been a carefully-thought-out plan to put me and the others off the scent," says Culme-Seymour, "but nothing will convince me of this."

The lunch, incidentally, was the last the two men had together; when the time came for the next one, Maclean was on the run.

"The only point that stood out that day was that Donald did not drink as much as usual," adds Culme-Seymour. "He spoke of wanting to indulge in a 'lost afternoon' around the pubs and clubs, but from his general demeanour I gathered that this was not a likely possibility. I was naturally rather pleased, for Donald when he was sober was a most charming and entertaining man."

There is yet another witness to support Culme-Seymour's opinion that Maclean, far from planning the flight weeks ahead, made up his mind on the spur of the moment. This man was a close friend of Maclean's who lunched with him the day before he left.

After the Foreign Secretary, Mr. Herbert Morrison, had made a statement in the House of Commons about the flight, this man wrote to him:

"I was very interested to read your remarks about Maclean and Burgess the other day, because I knew them both and actually lunched with Maclean the day before he disappeared. The point I wanted to mention to you was that on that day I am sure he had no intention of leaving in the way he did.

"He spoke to me so normally as to his private affairs, his wife's confinement and his plans for the immediate future that I am convinced that he was not then intending to leave the country. This makes me feel that, subsequent to meeting me on May 24th, he received some warning that he was under suspicion, and immediately left the country with Burgess. It may be, therefore, that someone in the Foreign Office told him on May 25th that you had authorised him to be questioned. Of course, it was not until the Foreign Office knew that the security service knew as well."

This letter is of great interest, but the last sentence makes a false assumption. The number of Foreign Office staff who knew of the investigation of Maclean and of its results was very small. It was M.I.5, in conjunction with Q, not the Foreign Office, who initiated it, and also issued specific instructions that as few people as possible were to be told (even Herbert Morrison has admitted that the disappearance was to him "a complete surprise").

And so it was not from the Foreign Office but from M.I.5 that the warning came, and it came not to Maclean but to Burgess. It came in a telephone call.

The Third Man was a senior member of the service who has since left and won honours in another field. He had been a close friend of Burgess, although he had not seen him for almost a year, and he was a homosexual. This is why it is nonsense to say that Burgess's homosexuality is irrelevant to the case, as, for instance, Tom Driberg claims in his book. It is irrelevant to moralise, certainly; but the fact remains that if he had *not* been a homosexual he would have been far less likely to have been warned of the danger to Maclean.

There is some reason to believe that Burgess will one day name the man publicly (in a book or when he returns to England), as he has already done privately. He has told many people that if he ever stands trial in Britain he will subpoena a number of well-known names for his defence, as well as two not-so-well-known ones— two of the friends who were then officers of M.I.5.

One of these two is the Third Man.

6

Day of Departure

BURGESS AND MACLEAN awoke that morning with no inkling of the dramatic events the day would bring.

Maclean caught his usual morning train, walked from Charing Cross to his office, said good-morning to the doorkeepers, hung up his hat and umbrella and settled down to work.

Burgess surfaced in more leisurely fashion. Since his suspension he had got into the habit of rising late, spending what was left of the morning pottering between his untidy, musty-smelling bedroom and the more comfortably furnished sitting-room. At 9.30 he was still in bed, the coverlet strewn with newspaper, stale cigarette-ends spilling out of an ash-tray, a Jane Austen novel on the floor, a cup of tea made by his flat-mate Jack Hewit in his hand.

Hewit went off to work, leaving Burgess attempting to find the address in Italy of W. H. Auden. He phoned Stephen Spender, a mutual friend, but could not reach him; he phoned other friends, but they did not know. He got up, bathed, shaved and dressed. At 10.30 he had an appointment with Bernard Miller to discuss the Paris trip that evening. He had not a care in the world; he had no ties, no job, no responsibilities of any kind. There were three hundred pounds in notes in the wardrobe, and a young man waiting for him round the corner. Life looked good.

But just after ten o'clock, he received a telephone call; a call that was to change his life irrevocably. It came from a friend in M.I.5, and told him that Maclean would be questioned on Monday. The necessary papers were going to the Foreign Office that day. . . .

Burgess hurried to Piccadilly, hailed a taxi and drove to the Green Park hotel to keep his appointment with Bernard Miller. They had coffee in the modestly-luxurious lounge and walked through Green Park. Miller was excited and talked animatedly for ten or fifteen minutes about Paris and the friends they would meet there. Half-way across the park, with the grey bulk of Buckingham Palace looming up through the trees, Burgess stopped and faced him. "Sorry Bernard," he said, "I haven't been listening, really. You see, a young friend at the Foreign Office is in serious trouble, and I have to help him out of it, somehow." This, incidentally, was the first time that Burgess mentioned the matter to anyone, even indirectly. Miller was astonished, not to say disappointed, but Burgess assured him that if he could still make the boat that night, he would—but that he would not be able to say anything definite until much later that day.

They parted just before twelve, each rather subdued, for different reasons.

Miller went back to his hotel, Burgess cutting through the park past Lord Rothermere's princely mansion, past what had been formerly the equally imposing town house of Lord Beaverbrook and out into St. James's Street. He was on his way to the Reform Club, to set in motion a chain of events which was to cost the Lords Rothermere and Beaverbrook something like a quarter of a million pounds. Ironically, it was Lord Beaverbrook's birthday the next day. . . .

At precisely that moment, Mr. Herbert Morrison was receiving two callers in his huge office in Whitehall. They brought with them a dossier of papers which the Foreign Secretary read gravely. He put his signature to one, and the visitors left. They now had the power to bring in Donald Maclean for questioning. . . .

As Burgess was entering the Reform, Maclean was on his way to Wheeler's to lunch with a young married couple. The place was crowded; they shared a dozen oysters and left. Maclean was in no hurry; his mind was untroubled. They went on to Schmidt's, in Charlotte Street, for two more courses. He accepted gratefully an offer from his friends to stay with them while Melinda was having the baby and promised to phone the next week.

He took a taxi to the Traveller's Club, had two drinks in the bar and cashed a cheque for five pounds, as he often did at week-ends. There was no one there he knew, and just after three he returned to his office. . . .

In the Reform, Burgess picked his way through the lounge to a corner armchair, slumped into it and thought deeply. Many people remember him like that, with a large whisky that he was hardly noticing, at his elbow. Half an hour went by. He spoke to no one. Then, calling the porter, he asked him to get Welbeck 3991 on the phone. This was the firm of Welbeck Motors, and from them he arranged to pick up a self-drive car. For how long did he want it? "Oh, ten days," he replied.

The switchboard then got him another London number, but afterwards the operator could not remember what it was. This call puzzled M.I.5 and the newspapers for weeks afterwards. Perhaps, they speculated, it held the key to the mystery. Who did he ring? Donald Maclean? His contact, whoever he was, at the Soviet Embassy? An agent or a helpful friend? Or the Third Man?

It was none of these. He phoned the Sunningdale number of an old university friend, whose wife answered. At her end of the line his voice was thick and incoherent. She put this down to drink, but she was puzzled, too, for he told her: "I'm going to do something which will shock you all, but don't worry about me. Don't worry." He would have gone on talking, but she had no interest in a drunken monologue when lunch was in the oven. She cut him short and hung up.

At ten past two, Burgess arrived in Crawford Street, Kensington, to collect his car. It was a cream Austin A70, registration number VMF 196. He paid £25 in cash (£15 hire, £10 deposit) and drove back to his flat. He called in at Gieves in Old Bond Street and bought a good quality fibre suitcase and a white macintosh. He saw Miller again, too, and told him that he would phone him or collect him at 8.30 that evening. At home, he carefully packed a tweed suit, several nylon shirts, shoes, socks, shaving kit and a dinner-jacket. He stuffed the three hundred pound notes and a bundle of savings certificates in his black official briefcase and carried them down to the car. As he went out, Hewit came in from the office. Burgess seemed preoccupied, said goodbye, and walked out. It was to be the last time the two men met.

At 4.45 precisely, Maclean emerged from the Foreign Office and walked the short distance to Charing Cross Station, soon to be lost in the hurrying throng of men who looked just like him: black bowlers, black jackets, briefcases and umbrellas. Many were making for the same train, the 5.19 to Sevenoaks. Two of the crowd were not travelling; the M.I.5 men that he knew were there, watching. They turned as he passed through the barrier and went back to their office, as they had done so often. It was the same every evening. But this was to be the end of their particular trail. . . .

Burgess arrived at Beaconshaw in his car barely half an hour after Maclean. The only help he could give his friend was to get him out of the country—and there were two boat tickets in his pocket. It can be conjectured that if Maclean had decided to go on his own, Burgess might well have driven back to London to keep his promise to Miller. But then, having given Maclean his boat ticket, he would not be able to go to Paris, though he *would* still have had the car. So it would have been easy for him to talk Miller into giving up the idea and going, say, to the Lake District instead—and, significantly, Burgess had actually asked for a map of the north of England in the Reform Club at lunch-time.

But whichever course Burgess took, Melinda would be questioned, and it would be dangerous if she said that Burgess had been there that night at the house. So she had better say that she had never seen her husband's friend before, and that he had been introduced to her as Roger Stiles. While the police were looking for Roger Stiles, Maclean would be out of the country, and he would be either safely with him or innocently holidaying with his friend in the north of England.

It was a plan which appealed in every aspect to Burgess with his schoolboy love of intrigue and the immense satisfaction which he got from a feeling that he was "riding the whirlwind and directing the storm".

Soon the three of them sat down to dinner. It was Maclean's birthday, and it must have been an extraordinary meal. It started at seven and was over by eight. By nine o'clock the two men were out of the house, their minds made up.

The story which Melinda asked M.I.5 to believe later was, indeed, that she did not know Burgess at all, and that her husband had introduced him as Roger Stiles, a colleague at the office. She found him a most charming and entertaining companion at dinner, she said, and they chatted about all kinds of subjects, certainly nothing to do with Communism, or Moscow.

When the meal was over, she went on, her husband had gone out into the garden to stoke up the central heating boiler. On his return he glanced at his watch and said that he had to go out with Mr. Stiles, but that they would not be gone long. No, she had no idea why they should have wanted to go out at that time of night, none at all. But she did not worry. She went to bed after tidying up the house (her relatives were arriving the next day) and slept. When did she expect her husband to return? Well, any time that night— although he *had* packed a few things, his razor and pyjamas, because, he told her, "we might have to spend the night somewhere".

Melinda said that she did not really worry until her guests had arrived the next day, and Donald had not even telephoned to explain his absence. Still, she said, he was a strange man; he did strange things, sometimes.

It was not until Monday that she made up her mind to telephone his office. In the afternoon, she spoke to Mr. G. A. Carey-Foster, the Chief Security Officer (head of "Q"), who told her not to worry—and not to talk about her husband's absence.

That was the outline of her story, and a very thin one it was, in retrospect even more so. After her initial call, however, her story mattered not at all to M.I.5.

What mattered was that the bird had flown, though how far had yet to be discovered.

After the initial shock which Melinda feigned, her life was in turmoil. Her first meeting with M.I.5 took place on the Wednesday following her husband's departure. It was in Lady Maclean's Piccadilly flat. Lady Maclean was in a state of shock, though, being a strong-willed woman, she managed to pull herself together to be as business-like as possible in the circumstances. Mr. Carey-Foster and two other men were there, as well as Melinda, who was treated with every sympathy and consideration, especially in view of her condition. The meeting was brief. Melinda was given no hint of what progress the security department had made, if any, and she was approached as though she, too, was a victim of what had happened, which, of course, she was, though perhaps not entirely an innocent one. Melinda answered questions in a very small voice, twisting and untwisting her gloves nervously, repeating constantly that she could not believe it. Again, she was advised not to worry, and not to discuss the matter. She called on her doctor, was given sedatives, and returned home.

On that day her mother, Mrs. Dunbar, came hurrying from France, aghast at the news that Melinda had given her by telephone the day before. There was nothing she could do, beyond comfort her daughter, and hope. . . .

On June 7, Melinda awoke to find that Donald's flight was a secret no longer. The *Daily Express* and, in the late edition, the *Daily Herald*, both carried front-page stories hinting at the scandal. There would obviously be no stopping them now. The next day, the two men were named in every newspaper in Britain. Her husband figured as the main news item on the early morning news bulletin, and by ten o'clock there was a long line of cars outside the house at Tatsfield. The local public-house was besieged with reporters when it opened its doors, and continued to do a brisk trade for very many days. Melinda all but barricaded herself in, refusing to answer questions or to meet the press in any way. That day was to bring another shock, totally unexpected. She received a telegram. It said:

"Mrs. Maclean Melinda. Beacon Shaw. Tatsfield near Westerham. Surrey England. Had to leave unexpectedly. Terribly sorry. Am quite well now. Don't worry darling I love you. Please don't stop loving me. Donald."

She phoned Lady Maclean immediately, to learn that she had received a similar message. She informed M.I.5 (who already knew) and gave a Special Branch man the telegram to study. Tracing it was a simple matter. Within an hour or two detectives learned that it had been handed in by a heavily-made-up woman at 10 p.m. the previous night, to a post office in the Place de la Bourse, Paris.

One mystery which defies explanation even today is apparent in a *Daily Telegraph* report of June 9:

"It was learned in Paris last night that the text released there of the telegram sent to Mr. Maclean's wife is an abbreviated version. The full text contained eighty-two words. The French Authorities declined to explain why they omitted the missing words."

Heavy-handed censorship might have accounted for the strangeness of the wording.

Incidentally, Burgess's mother was not forgotten. A telegram to her, sent from Rome, read:

"Terribly sorry for my silence. Am embarking on long Mediterranean holiday. Do forgive. Guy."

At least the English was better. . . .

The Austin sped down the winding country lanes from Westerham, its headlights picking out the signposts that led to Southampton, 100 miles on. They were late, and it looked likely that all their plans would collapse through missing the midnight boat to St. Malo.

On the back seat were the suitcases, two of Burgess's, (and his briefcase), and one of Maclean's. The conversation in the car can only be imagined; Maclean, no doubt, depressed at the thought of leaving his wife in a terrifying predicament, Burgess elated at the prospect of excitement. There was no going back now; it had all been finally settled in such a hurry that, for, perhaps, the first time in his life, he had deliberately missed an appointment (with Miller) and, uncharacteristically, not even telephoned to apologise. They arrived in Southampton at 11.45, fifteen minutes before the boat sailed. Burgess had to leave the car at the dockside, unlocked.

On board the *Falaise*, they went straight to their cabin and did not appear in the bar at all. Next morning, they disembarked at 10.30 in the pouring rain on the grey quayside of St. Malo. Burgess left behind, under his bed, the suitcase containing his dinner-jacket. He would not need that where he was going.

They had already decided to make for Rennes, but missed the train by minutes. At the station they caught a taxi and ordered Albert Gilbert, the incredulous driver, to Rennes, miles away. He drove as only French taxi-drivers can, and beat the train by twenty minutes. From there to Paris, from Paris, on the night express, to Berne. They sat in the station restaurant until the Czech Consulate Visa Section opened, and had their passports stamped for Prague, where an international trade fair had opened. By train to Zurich, then by plane to Prague, with two days' waiting in between. This, anyway, is the now-officially-accepted story of their flight, and as far as it could be checked, it has been, with one snag.

Burgess has claimed on several occasions that they stayed in an hotel in Berne, but could not remember the name (and Swiss intelligence checked very soon afterwards) and not one possessed an aliens card in the names of Burgess and Maclean. And of all the countries in the world where (especially in those days) it was necessary for a foreigner to produce his passport at an hotel, Switzerland was the strictest. Therefore, they had either false passports, or else stayed at a "safe" house or, perhaps, an embassy.

Two days before Maclean's third child was born, he and Burgess stepped off an airliner and on to Russian soil. The bridges behind them were burning fiercely. . . .

7

And Now, Melinda

It must have been with some relief that on June 13, Melinda entered hospital. Even the Caesarean operation she had to undergo, she joked later, was worth the few days' peace she had then. In the hours that she had to wait in the labour ward, Melinda wrote this letter:

My dearest Donald:

If you ever receive this letter, it will mean that I shan't be here to tell you how much I love you and how really proud of you I am. My only regret is that perhaps you don't know how I feel about you.

I feel I leave behind and have had a wonderful gift in your love and the existence of Fergie and Donald. I am so looking forward to the new baby. It seems strangely like the first time and I really think I shall enjoy this baby completely. I never forget, darling, that you love me and am living for the moment when we shall all be together again.

All my deepest love and wishes for a happy life for you and the children.

Melinda

Clearly this was written with deep sincerity and emotion, and with the stark fact facing her that the operation might cost her her life. One sentence is revealing, in the light of her protestations of ignorance: ". . . how really proud of you I am". Whatever the assessment of her husband, it is impossible not to admire and respect Melinda, a woman of tremendous courage with deep convictions, who faced far greater dangers than Maclean, acting with the cunning and spirit of a lioness defending her young.

That letter was never posted. She eventually left it behind for her mother to find among her personal papers, twenty-seven months later.

On the morning of June 13 she gave birth to a healthy girl, and recovered completely and quickly. With the baby she seemed to renew her strength, and faced the inevitable reporters defiantly (though still telling them nothing). She said nothing, on direct instructions from the Foreign Office; she told friends that she would not have minded one press conference if a bargain could have been made that she would be left in peace afterwards. This is an old bargain that has often been made by Fleet Street, and often (though not always) adhered to by newspapers.

The pressure on her from both the press and security men began to build up, as neither body was getting anywhere with their separate enquiries. Mrs. Dunbar, fearing that her daughter would have a nervous breakdown, found and rented a house at Beauvallon, near St. Tropez, towards the end of July.

Another bombshell came just before the move, in the form of two drafts for £1,000, sent on Maclean's behalf from Switzerland. They went to Mrs. Dunbar; to Melinda went a letter from Donald. It was warm, affectionate and apologetic, and from the moment she received it, it was never out of her handbag.

Melinda and her three children set off for the south of France on August 17 with her mother, her sister Catherine and Catherine's child. They went against the advice of the Foreign Office and M.I.5, but Mrs. Dunbar insisted, and as the journey was genuinely for health reasons the objections were withdrawn. For the first ten days, the villa was besieged with reporters and photographers, but they were gradually withdrawn until the whole family were left in peace for their last fortnight.

Melinda wrote to Harriet, back in England:

"Life goes on and gradually a pattern seems to emerge out of the swamp. Oh, I can't tell you how completely shipwrecked I feel. Like a drowning man, my past seems to rise up and confront me and I couldn't be more horrified. I made the fatal mistake of reading old letters (1939 ones, not Donald's) and as far as I can see I never wrote and answered any of them and altogether behaved so bitchily or unconsciously that it isn't true. I can't tell you how shocked I am." She ended: ". . . nor have I lost a particle of faith in Donald, but, oh, God, why is life quite so difficult?"

With almost a year of separation gone and still not knowing where her husband was for certain, she spoke to friends of divorce, but "discovered" that under English law she would have to wait three years before obtaining grounds of desertion. It seems unlikely that she did not know this already, but even to friends there could be no let-up in the pretence.

The move to Switzerland made the Soviet intelligence operation that was to come, much easier.

Remembering what happened the previous year, Melinda asked the Foreign Office for permission to issue a press statement. It went to the Press Association, and stated that she intended to live in France or Switzerland for the sake of greater privacy for the children.

There were no assurances from the press that she would be left alone, but one was volunteered by M.I.5, who also reported that they had no indications yet of where Burgess and Maclean were.

The beginning of September found the family in Geneva, with a small home in the Rue des Alpes. The two boys started school, and life returned to normal, temporarily. Apart from one quick trip back to England to do some Christmas shopping and see old friends, Melinda lay low. On January 1, 1953, she wrote to Harriet again:

"Thank God for the New Year. I couldn't be happier to see 1952 go. Mother and I celebrated quietly with a bottle of champagne and a miniature log fire and in our strange optimistic way we felt that perhaps 1953 might be better for us all. We survived Christmas once more. I am really getting to dread it and Mother and I could hardly wait to throw away all the Christmas decorations; only the tree remains. Next year I am going to send the boys away with their school friends on a skiing trip."

It could be that hope was fading for Melinda now; the hope that it would be possible to join Donald in Russia. Anyway, she discussed with her mother at great length the possibility of going to live at home again in America. Mrs. Dunbar was delighted at the prospect, and hurried off to New York with two principal objectives: to see if Melinda's American passport could be renewed, and to enquire about the possibilities of a divorce for her there. It was to be a wasted journey.

While she was away, Melinda was contacted by an agent of the NVD. Swiss intelligence believe this man was an American, who passed through Geneva very quickly, stopping only long enough to brief Melinda on the plan to get her out. On his instructions, she called on a photographer's shop in Geneva and had passport pictures made of herself and the children. She wanted them in a hurry, she said, and gave her name as Mrs. Smith. The reason for the hurry was that her mother was already on her way back from New York, and actually arrived three days later, to be told nothing of this development, of course.

The agent may have chosen the meeting-place, and if so, it is likely to have been the tiny skiing resort of Saanenmoser, near Gstaad, where she went with the children for two weeks. This is a probability only because, as we will see, she returned there later, for no good reason.

Mrs. Dunbar was horrified at the change in her daughter on her return; she was strained, with a white face and the listlessness that she had shown in England. Her health, it appeared, had suffered a major setback. Gone was the excitement at the prospect of living in America again; she read only casually the papers and forms her mother had carefully collected in order to smooth away her problems.

The one incident which brought her alive again was the offer from a friend of a holiday villa in Majorca. Arrangements were made for them all to move there on July 1, but, unaccountably, two or three days before, Melinda changed her mind and cancelled everything, much to the dismay of Mrs. Dunbar and the anguish of the children.

Instead, she announced calmly, she was taking the boys to Saanenmoser, instead of Majorca! There was no snow and nothing else to do there. What on earth did she want to go to Saanenmoser for? "Mountain air", her daughter replied.

On the day she should have arrived in Palma, Melinda and her baby daughter and two unhappy boys drove off on their improbable holiday. "Back in a fortnight" were her last words to her mother.

But she was back in five days. The weather had been bad; she had been completely mistaken, explained Melinda, adding that she would like nothing better than to now make the Majorcan trip.

They did, and the five weeks they spent there in the sun made a tremendous difference to all of them.

The message arrived on the day that they returned to Geneva—on Monday, September 7. According to the Swiss authorities Melinda went to the central post office and collected a Poste Restante letter. It informed her that the operation to smuggle her out would take place in three days' time.

That afternoon, she wandered around as if in a daze. Mrs. Dunbar, by now accustomed to her daughter's extraordinary moods, said nothing, but watched anxiously. Melinda went shopping for items that were unnecessary, and spent the evening writing letters to people she had not written to for months.

As they were going to bed that night, Melinda stood in the doorway between their rooms. Mrs. Dunbar thought she looked ill and worried. Suddenly, she said: "Oh, how I wish I had someone to advise me!" Her mother wondered if she were referring to the sale of the Tatsfield house which they had been discussing earlier in the day. She told Melinda she had some experience with property and asked if she could help. Melinda just shook her head and shut the bedroom door.

Melinda appeared to be quite normal on Friday morning, September 11. She had breakfast and went out shopping. From her bank she drew out 700 Swiss francs (£58), and paid the rent of the flat. She also paid a £5 repair bill on her car at the Fleury garage, telling the mechanic to fill the petrol tank. At 11 a.m. she returned to the flat and told her mother that she had met a man called Robin Muir, a friend from Cairo, in the market. He had invited her and the children to spend a week-end with him and his wife at their villa in Territet. He had explained that she might have difficulty in finding the villa but would meet her in the lobby of a Montreux hotel at 4.30 that afternoon.

The boys wore grey flannel suits and blue sports shirts, the baby was dressed in a new coat and shoes, Melinda wore a bright blue, three-quarter length Schiaparelli coat, and at 3.30 p.m. they were ready to go. They would be back, said Melinda, on Sunday evening because the boys had to go to school on Monday morning at 8.15. Melinda asked if she should telephone her mother when they arrived at Territet. Mrs. Dunbar told her it was unnecessary; she would only be away a couple of days.

Melinda was quite calm as she left with two suitcases and the children. There was nothing in her demeanour to indicate prior knowledge of the fantastic step she was taking. Mrs. Dunbar waved them goodbye and said she would be waiting for them on Sunday and Melinda drove off with the three keys to the flat and the only key to the letter box.

Mrs. Dunbar laid the table for tea at 6 o'clock on Sunday and then sat at the window looking out for their car. The hours went by. Mrs. Dunbar became frantic with worry, particularly as Melinda had not even telephoned to explain their delay. But, perhaps, the roads were choked with traffic and they had decided to delay their return until Monday morning. She tried to console herself with this thought but spent a very disturbed night.

With no news of them on the Monday, Mrs. Dunbar went to the British consulate and explained what had happened. The reaction there was only irritating: she was told that her report of their absence would go through ordinary channels. She tried to get the officials to appreciate the urgency of the situation. She failed.

Back to the flat went Mrs. Dunbar and put through a call to the Chief Security Officer at the Foreign Office. The result was immediate. Two senior M.I.5 men were flown out to Geneva, the Swiss police were alerted, and the search began.

The following day, a telegram was delivered to Mrs. Dunbar. Handed in at Territet and written in a foreign handwriting containing several errors, it said:

"Terribly sorry delay in contacting you—unforeseen circumstances have arisen am staying here longer please advise school boys returning about a weeks time—all extremely well—pink rose in marvellous form—love from all—Melinda."

Melinda's black Chevrolet car was found next morning forty miles from Geneva, in a Lausanne garage only a few hundred yards from the station. The police were told by the garage proprietor that the car had been left there by a woman with three children about 7 p.m. on the Friday that Melinda disappeared. A piece of paper stuck under the windscreen wiper said it would be collected in seven days.

The car was dirty, the speedometer broken, the cigarette lighter pulled out and left hanging down, and the battery was flat. Among the articles in the car were a cardboard box from a Geneva patisserie, the remains of a packed meal, road maps, and children's toys.

There was also a children's book on the front seat of the car. Its title: *Little Lost Lamb*. Inside the cover was stamped: "Property of Norwalk Conn Schools, Washington School". It was a book that Mrs. Dunbar had never seen before.

The preface said: "When the little black lamb scrambled up the mountainside by himself, he didn't think he would get lost. He was only having fun exploring. But when it was time to go home, there was no little lamb among all the other sheep. Then came a cry which the shepherd knew meant danger for all little lambs away from their mothers. . . ."

Perhaps this was meant to be Melinda's last message. She was certainly a little lost lamb and she certainly scrambled up a mountainside into the unknown when she left her mother in Geneva.

Melinda caught the 6.58 p.m. train from Lausanne to Zurich—a ticket collector at the station and a Swiss professor remembered seeing her and the children catch it. An American colonel shared a first-class compartment with them on the night train from Zurich to the Austrian town of Schwarzach St. Veit, forty miles from Salzburg. A porter there remembered them leaving the train at 9 a.m. on the Saturday. He said they went into a restaurant for coffee and about half an hour later they were driven away in a big American car. The driver was described as a slim man of medium height who spoke German with an Austrian accent.

There the trail ended. No one saw her after that.

For four days after Melinda's disappearance, Mrs. Dunbar was too distraught to sleep. The initial shock was followed by realisation of the significance of her daughter's disappearance: that she might never see Melinda and her grandchildren again; that the Iron Curtain had shut them out of her life for ever. She felt beaten and exhausted and left for Paris to seek consolation from her daughter, Harriet.

Five weeks later she returned to Geneva to close the flat in the Rue des Alpes. Nothing seemed to have been touched in her absence, but when she began looking for Melinda's clothes she found nearly everything had gone. Coats, suits, dresses, blouses, sweaters, cardigans, skirts, shoes and underclothing—they were all missing. Only her mink coat and an expensive new evening dress were left in the wardrobe.

Someone could have been sent to the flat while Mrs. Dunbar was away in Paris to pack Melinda's clothes and take them to her—she had the keys to the flat with her when she disappeared. But this would have meant gambling on the flat not being watched by the police and risking the possibility of being seen by the concierge. The more feasible explanation is that Melinda knew well in advance that she was joining Maclean in Russia and packed everything she could.

Mrs. Dunbar closed up the flat and went sadly back

to her daughter in Paris. There, at the end of October, she received a short letter from Melinda. It had been posted in Cairo on October 24 and was written on cheap, greyish-blue notepaper.

It began: "Darling Mummy"—the usual way in which Melinda began letters to her mother.

Melinda said she and the children were safe and well and she hoped her mother would understand how deeply she felt the sorrow and worry her departure would cause her. They all missed Mrs. Dunbar and would always think of her. She sent their love to her and to Catherine and Harriet.

"Please believe me, darling, in my heart I could not have done otherwise than I have done," she wrote.

The letter ended: "Goodbye—but not for ever. Melinda."

8

Paperchase

THE PRESSES of Fleet Street devoured every word of the Burgess and Maclean story from the start, showing an appetite—and a lack of table manners—that shocked successive British governments, embarrassed the Foreign Office and thoroughly discomfited the security services.

Why? Why *did* the newspapers create such a fuss?

It was, as I have said, the time of the crumbling Image. There was a feeling in Britain, as distinctive as the atmosphere of the thirties; a sick apprehension and uncertainty, a lack of direction and a suspicion and fear which added up to a national neurosis. The wildest weed of rumour flowered at speed, with only the lightest overnight watering of fact necessary. The very thought of two British diplomats fleeing to the Russians with an unknown quantity of secrets was enough to send shivers down Britannia's spine. Anxiety was heightened by the government policy of telling as little as possible, like a doctor with a deeply suspicious patient saying there is not much wrong.

The British press determined to find out what *was* wrong, and mounted one of the largest operations ever undertaken by Fleet Street. Overall, it was the biggest story of the century.

It broke on the morning of June 6, 1951. Into the

office of the *Daily Express* went a curious, intriguing tip: two Foreign Office men had vanished, and were believed to be behind the Iron Curtain. That was all. The source cannot be named, but those who know his identity have speculated many times, since, on the reasons for passing on this information so gratuitously. However, the message was enough to alert, through the Foreign desk, *Express* correspondents in Paris, Rome, Vienna and Prague. By mid-afternoon, though, their enquiries had produced nothing. On the editorial conference schedule, the item remained, starkly, "Foreign Office mystery". The hours ticked away on the wall-clocks of the huge news-room, and the story was almost forgotten under the pressure of another one which occupied more than half the front page: a young gunman, Alan Poole, was holding 200 armed police at bay in his home at Chatham.

Then, at 10 p.m., Larry Solon, chief of the Paris bureau, spoke to the night editor. His brief report caused a hurried conference and a major change in the make-up of Page One. Within half an hour there was an open line to Paris, and reporters were seeking out contacts all over London.

The enquiries went on all night—to the annoyance of many civil servants whose phones rang hours after they were asleep. But in ten hours there was little progress. The paper's front page that morning carried only four paragraphs; four dramatic paragraphs though that scooped the world. They said, simply:

"Scotland Yard officers and French detectives are hunting for two British government employees who are believed to have left London with the intention of getting to Moscow.

"According to a friend they planned the journey 'to serve their idealistic purposes'. One report says that the two men were employed by the Foreign Office and that there is a possibility that they may have important papers with them.

"News of their plan was given to the authorities by a friend, who said they expected him to go with them. They were to go to France as if on holiday, and make their way behind the Iron Curtain. The friend backed out.

"Several experts have flown from London to France to work with the French police. All French airports and frontiers are being watched. Plain-clothes men are searching the Montmartre area of Paris, where it is easy for anyone to hide. It is understood the police are watching visitors to the Soviet Embassy in Paris."

That was the start of the hunt. It is worthwhile to read that first report again, remembering that the reporters who worked through the night met with nothing but bland denials or blank faces or furious accusations of scandal-mongering. "Nonsense . . . completely untrue . . . rubbish . . ." were the official replies. Early the following morning came the first Foreign Office statement, forced by Solon's story:

"Two members of the Foreign Service have been

missing from their homes since May 25. One is Mr. D. D. Maclean, the other Mr. G. F. de M. Burgess. All possible enquiries are being made. It is known that they went to France a few days ago. Mr. Maclean had a breakdown a year ago owing to overstrain, but was believed to have fully recovered. Owing to their being absent without leave, both have been suspended with effect from June 1."

The first incredible fact to emerge from the story—after the release of the names of the diplomats—was the fact that Melinda Maclean was pregnant. It seemed fantastic that a Foreign Office diplomat, ex-public-schoolboy and all that, should desert his wife so callously a few weeks or even days before the birth of their baby.

Excitement in Fleet Street offices was tremendous; it seemed abundantly clear that there was enough dirt and incompetence on high to merit the most searching examination of every factor that led up to the scandal.

As each fragment of the tale unfolded, day by day, week by week, month by month, and—incredibly—year by year, it was obvious that much was being glossed over if not actually suppressed by the authorities. It began to look as though the powers-that-be were frightened of what might come out—so newspapermen pressed even harder for the truth.

All the resources of Fleet Street were thrown into the coverage of the story, and at one time or another most of the general reporters, crime reporters, political and defence correspondents worked on it. The *Express* offered £1,000 reward for news of the two men. Its great rival, the *Daily Mail*, raised the figure later to £10,000. Executives of the *Express* today estimate that they spent more than £100,000 over the years on the story, in everything from tips to the doormen of hotels to first-class air fares to Moscow. Unquestionably, the Burgess and Maclean scandal remained the *Express*'s story throughout.

"Our great scoop," says Morley Richards today, "was Beaverbrook's own.

"I don't know how he got it, but it was magnificent. He called the office one night to say that Mrs. Maclean had been paid a large amount of money from her husband in Moscow, via a Swiss bank. We checked at great length, and managed to get enough to print it. What a row that caused! It was worth the £1,000 we paid to Lord Beaverbrook's contact to get it, anyway."

The story of that "large amount of money" is interesting. The cheques were sent by the Swiss Bank Corporation and the Union Bank of Switzerland on the instructions of a Mr. Robert Becker, who said he was staying at the Hotel Central in Zurich. He gave a home address in New York. He looked, said a cashier later, like an ordinary American tourist-businessman. Swiss police called at the Hotel Central and drew a blank; no one of that name had stayed there. The cashiers were taken to the hotel and watched the guests going in and out without recognising their quarry.

The F.B.I. in New York reported that the address of "Mr. Becker" was non-existent. Mrs. Dunbar told

M.I.5 she had never heard of anyone of that name. Nor had Lady Maclean or Melinda. Only the money was real.

The letter that arrived at the same time was posted in Guildford, Surrey, a fact which helped not at all. For the newspapers the whole affair was a splendid mystery; for M.I.5 it was a sharp and unwelcome spur, particularly as it was a public one, originated by a newspaper that was highly critical of their efforts.

All through the background story of the investigation into the disappearance of Burgess and Maclean, however, runs the disturbing fact that had it not been for newspaper revelations such as this—and many others besides —the public would still be in ignorance of many official shortcomings.

An interesting example can be found in the case of Mrs. Maclean's disappearance. From the beginning, from the day that her husband vanished, Melinda was a figure of mystery; partly self-made mystery, understandably. She shut herself away in her home, refused to be interviewed or photographed, and made statements only through third parties—and then only to complain bitterly of the behaviour of Fleet Street men. With injured innocence, she proclaimed that she was being hounded unjustly; she knew nothing and could not help. The security services eventually believed her and with gallant English deference to her pregnancy called off the half-hearted watch that had been kept on her house.

Not so the press. For months there was always a reporter somewhere in the vicinity of Tatsfield; all convinced that one day she would lead them to news of her husband. "Won't the bloody press *ever* let this drop?" she asked in a letter to one of her relatives.

The bloody press would not. "Undoubtedly," says Morley Richards, "she knew of the plot from the start— I think everyone at the *Express* believed that. But the attack to which we were subjected on the issue of the intrusion into her privacy inhibited our efforts. Had not so many members of the Establishment taken up the cudgels for her so fiercely she would not have got away."

From all the commotion over intrusion there came the decision of a dozen editors to leave the story alone, unless there were startling developments. Melinda Maclean was followed and photographed at the start of her holiday in France, to be sure (Geoffrey Hoare was very critical of this in his book), but in the end there was not a reporter within miles when the couple established contact with each other again. Not a single reporter, and not a single secret serviceman.

This peeved the British government, which stated in the White Paper: "From information subsequently received from witnesses in Switzerland and Austria, it seems clear that the arrangements for Mrs. Maclean's departure from Geneva had been carefully planned . . ."

Certainly no one in Fleet Street was surprised at the evidence of "careful planning". They had pointed out for more than a year that Donald Maclean had *someone* working for him in Switzerland and actually sending large amounts of cash from there to his wife in London!

The row over the "intrusion" broke soon after the

disclosure of the funds sent to Melinda from Moscow.

It followed the Press Association statement on July 15, 1952: "Mrs. Melinda Maclean is shortly proceeding to France with her children to spend a holiday of some weeks there.

"In accordance with the practice she has adopted since the disappearance of her husband Mrs. Maclean has notified the Foreign Office of her intentions.

"She is hoping, it is learned, by changing her residence, to ensure a degree of privacy for her family of young children."

The men around the big news desk of the *Express* gave a concerted horse-laugh. George Joyce, one of the most experienced reporters, was assigned to interview her immediately.

He did—on the telephone. But in the story which appeared next morning there were the dangerous words: "Mrs. Maclean smiled. . . ." Something he patently could not have seen on the telephone.

It was a bad slip, but the repercussions were far more serious than he expected.

Every enemy of the newspapers—and of the *Express* in particular—flew into a righteous rage at this 'typical' example of newspaper villainy. From here it was only a step to condemning the whole interview as fiction. Mrs. Maclean fanned the flames by making an appeal for privacy and condemning the reporters and photographers (never identified) for badgering her children on the way home from school. Letters appeared in *The Times* expressing disgust at this shameful treatment of a poor woman who had, obviously and unwittingly, been the victim of circumstances. *She* was not responsible for her husband's defection; *she* knew nothing about it; *she* was whiter than white. Public sympathy grew and the flood of protesting letters that poured into the *Express* office left no doubt that many people felt strongly enough to cancel their subscriptions.

The row was still going on when Mrs. Maclean slipped out of the country and made the secret contacts with Donald through agents in Switzerland. . . .

One man who watched her go with mixed feelings was Donald Seaman, a reporter who today has the unique distinction of being able to claim that he has spent eleven years on the story—"and for five of them I did very little else". Seaman, well known in Fleet Street for his sheer dogged persistence on stories, needed all his patience on this one.

Twenty-four hours after Solon's four paragraphs appeared on Page One Seaman was sitting in the news room typing a weather story. He had fifteen minutes to finish it before catching the last train home from King's Cross. Handing in the copy to the night editor he was asked: "Can you speak Italian?" "A little," he answered. "I was there for a couple of years during the war."

He was a trifle wary about giving this much away; with one eye on the clock, he felt that he was probably going to be asked to speak to an Italian waiter in a Soho café. Instead, he caught the next flight to Rome. The *Express* had learned of Burgess's attempts to discover the address in Italy of Auden. Arthur Christiansen, the editor, wondered why a man about to head for Moscow (if the rumours were true) should choose a time like that to enquire about friends in Italy. Seaman was sent to the sunshine island of Ischia to find out.

Auden did not know, and said so. But he had some revealing things to say about his old friend Guy Burgess. "Guy was a Communist in the late 1930s," he told Seaman, "and he was still pro-Communist when he was at the British Embassy in Washington." This was new to the public. He also disclosed that Alan Nunn May, the atom spy, had been a close friend and fellow under-graduate of the missing diplomat.

Seaman dictated that first interview to his office in London as the famous poet sat by his side in a crowded wine-shop that held the only telephone in the village of Forio. He paid thousands of lire to keep the line open (it normally shut down at 6 p.m.) and shouted every word through the din of an Italian peasants' night out. That scene was similar to many Seaman took part in during the next few months, as the Burgess and Maclean story took him to almost every country in Europe. He was joined by George Joyce—now with Cable and Wireless. While Seaman concentrated on Burgess, Joyce became the authority on Maclean.

Both reporters believed that the storm which broke over Melinda Maclean's "intrusion" complaints was really serving as a smokescreen to cover her escape to Europe and eventual reunion with her husband.

Seaman pleaded with Christiansen to be allowed to

follow her to Switzerland. His plan—admittedly an expensive one—was to take a flat somewhere near her and watch and wait. He expected it to take months and bet colleagues that her next move would come within a year.

"Donald was one of my best reporters," says Christiansen now, "and I was faced with a dilemma. I knew that if there was going to be a story, he would get it. I believed, as he did, that she would eventually disappear too. I desperately wanted the *Express* to have that story when it broke. But I had to put all this against the cost of keeping a good man there, out of action for maybe a year. Then, too," he smiled, "there was the human element; how much did Donald just want to live in Switzerland for a bit?"

Seaman lost his fight, anyway, but his prophecy came true. Melinda vanished just a year later.

That year was filled with many more excitements. Colin Valdar, the brilliant young features editor of the *Express* (and later editor of the *Sunday Pictorial* and the *Daily Sketch*) had the idea of hiring Col. Oreste Pinto, the wartime "Spycatcher".

Pinto has said that he hated taking the job on at the time. "The trail was cold, and one year old; what did they expect me to do?" Once more, Seaman was picked for the job; to accompany Pinto everywhere and write the reports. The operation became, in the words of an *Express* sub-editor at the time, "a bloody uproar from start to finish". Pinto was a swashbuckling type who enjoyed living and enjoyed cloak-and-dagger living particularly, though he lost no opportunity to din into Seaman that the whole quest was hopeless. "I have none of my wartime authority," he said. "I'm not sure about my old contacts now and I've got virtually no clues."

Nevertheless, he led Seaman on a breathless chase across Europe. They were joined by a new acquisition of the newspaper—Jack Hewit, the ex-room-mate of Burgess.

This somewhat improbable trio used every known means of transport to cover five countries, hunting for a lead. Pinto phoned the *Express* frequently in great excitement; "Usually," recalls Morley Richards, "to ask for more money to be sent out." Eventually the news editor sent Seaman a cable in Vienna: "Forget Burgess and Maclean. Find Pinto."

Amid all the laughter and the cynicism, however, there was a serious side which could not be printed. The wide publicity that Pinto's search was receiving—not only in the *Express* but in the Continental papers—made him a marked man. At several points, particularly in Switzerland and Vienna, he crossed the path of the diplomats, and came into contact with people who, it later transpired, had certainly been "in the know". On three occasions he was warned by telephone to keep his nose out of other people's business. It needed no imagination to guess who the people were and what their business was.

Pinto later said that he felt himself hamstrung. He could not afford to ignore the threats, but he could not afford to dig deeper and follow them up, either; he was working for a commercial organisation, not a government department. A great deal of material that he unearthed was written by him in a confidential memo and read only by a few of the *Express* executives. Valdar today says: "There is no doubt that Pinto was on to something big when we stopped the operation; it was big enough to be too hot to handle."

Hewit's participation was another profitless venture. As a contact he was unique; because of his special friendship with Burgess he knew him in some ways better than his family. He was willing to help the investigation—up to a point—and he knew the identity of almost everyone who had called at Burgess's flat. But Burgess, an inveterate letter-writer, failed utterly to get in touch with Hewit, as the *Express* team hoped that he might. And Hewit quickly lost many of his friends, angering them by committing the unforgivable sin of talking to the newspapers. Actually, they were being prudent, and he was not. To be publicly listed as a friend of either diplomat brought a man or woman under the eyes of the smarting security servicemen. For anyone to have visited Burgess or Maclean, however innocently, in the days or hours before their disappearance was to court searching enquiry, if not suspicion. No one wanted to talk.

Seaman once waited three weeks outside a flat in London trying to speak to a man who—so he had been told—had called on Burgess in the early hours of May 24, the day of the flight. Eventually he caught his man, only to be told: "I have nothing to say. Go to the authorities."

But the authorities had nothing to say either. It was back to the office, to sort wearily through the monster postbags that brought the daily response to the offer of £1,000 reward. The letters came from London, Liverpool, Marseilles and Middlesborough, Salcombe and La Spezia, all tipping off, enquiring, kidding, guessing, hoping. They were fortune-tellers and fortune-seekers, water-diviners and cranks, mischief-makers and others genuinely mistaken. There may even have been a genuine witness among them, but try as they could reporters could not find him.

Seaman—and Percy Hoskins—today are still on the story; no single new development occurs that is not fully considered, digested, checked, double-checked and filed by them. This has been routine since that night in June 1951. Hoskins is a walking encyclopedia on the mystery. This year he headed the big team of Expressmen who flew out to Amsterdam to await the rumoured return home of the diplomats though, as he says, he had no real hopes of seeing them.

Seaman has travelled to France, Italy, Norway, Sweden, Denmark, Finland, Austria, Czechoslovakia, the Middle East, Switzerland and twice to the Soviet Union on this assignment. He began asking questions about Burgess and Maclean when he was in his twenties and is still asking them at 39. He was once asked what he thought he had achieved. "As far as I am concerned," he replied, "the eleven years are a failure—they don't mean a thing until Maclean tells the truth and nothing but the truth."

The Russian press, understandably, was silent on the matter of the Soviet Union's latest acquisition. Every Russian diplomat who ever attended a cocktail party in the West was asked about the pair, but all feigned complete ignorance. Mr. Kruschev himself, in answer to repeated questions from Western correspondents, denied point blank that they were in the Soviet Union.

This was followed up, on October 4, 1953, by an article in the magazine *New Times*, the Communists' *New Statesman*. The whole affair of Burgess and Maclean, it said, was typical of the West's "shameless methods of poisoning the international atmosphere. The campaign around the disappearance of Maclean is clearly inspired by the ruling circles of the Imperialist states," it went on, adding authoritatively: "Insignificant in itself and having not the slightest relationship to the Soviet Union, the childish affair of the swindlers of the capitalist press, intelligence and diplomacy is an attempt to confuse international political events with the clear aim of arousing empty and even absurd suspicions among the most confident English, French and Swiss minds, and muddying the waters in order to fish out anti-Soviet fish."

It is hard not to compare this slightly inaccurate report with George Joyce's error in stating that Mrs. Maclean smiled down a telephone. The editor of the *New Times* no doubt received official congratulations for publishing his huge lie; George Joyce was all but sacked.

For everyone, coverage of this story called for un-limited patience. For example, it took the *Express seven years* from the date of first application to get Seaman his first visa to enter Russia. And by that time the diplomats had given an interview anyway.

Other offices were faring no better; all were spending thousands of pounds, much of it on wild goose chases. One Russian émigré with a plausible story boasts today of having received £100 from three newspapers for a tip-off never published. Normally editors are canny, cautious men, but this story had got under their skins.

The displeasure of the Establishment was immense and intimidating. The *Sunday Dispatch* dared to say that Burgess had "strong Communist tendencies" while in America; this was quoted by Sir Jocelyn Lucas, M.P., in the House of Commons, and brought this reply from Herbert Morrison: "With great respect, I would not take any notice."

It was an unfortunate phrase; the newspaper stories were making it abundantly clear that the two men had for years been unreliable, irresponsible, homosexual and terrifying security risks—but that for some reason, nobody *had* taken any notice. Every national newspaper suggested this, and it is safe to say that every national newspaper found itself in trouble with influential officials for saying so. The atmosphere at Foreign Office press conferences was as cold as yesterday's teapot.

Whatever the pros and cons of the endless arguments between journalists and officialdom, it was, nevertheless, the press who prodded the government into activity, unearthed many of the clues, established and announced the whereabouts of the two men . . . and even found them in a Moscow hotel.

This particular incident is one of the most fascinating episodes in the background story of Burgess and Maclean. It is a remarkable tribute to a reporter's tenacity and initiative.

The reappearance of the missing pair, as abrupt and dramatic as their flight, took newspapermen and diplomats alike completely off-balance—with the exception perhaps of one correspondent.

There have been other times, and other places, where the influence of informed newspapermen has had a decisive effect on government policies, although this is not a popular notion.

At this time—February 1956—and in this place—Moscow—the man was Richard Hughes, the renowned, much-travelled correspondent of the *Sunday Times*.

Hughes had been in Moscow for ten weeks on a wide-ranging assignment covering the progress and prospects of the new Five Year Plan, and the meeting of the Supreme Soviet. And, like every other reporter, he also had the general briefing: "See if you can find out anything, anything at all, about Those Two."

It did not take him long to discover that all the resident correspondents in Moscow were being constantly prodded by their home offices for the same thing. Nor did it take him long to become as frustrated, furious and frantic as they were.

Any enquiries to officialdom were either forgotten or lost—or met with the bland but definite assurance that nobody knew anything.

This polite, brick-wall tactic, so much more efficient

and infuriating than any Iron Curtain, was the end of every conversation with even the most carefully developed contacts.

Mr. Kruschev himself denied that he knew anything at all about the missing men.

There was nothing. Nothing at all. Blank. Nil. Niet.

Or was there perhaps just *one* possibility?

Kruschev and Bulganin were shortly due to make their famous B & K visit to England and it was known they had high hopes of it. They wanted the best possible atmosphere to greet their arrival. It was essential that there be no rough patches that could not be smoothed over beforehand. They hoped for a great personal success and an increase in goodwill all round, especially after recent anti-colonial speeches by Mr. K had been so sourly received.

To Richard Hughes, worrying at the problem in his room at Moscow's National Hotel, it seemed likely that B & K had been misinformed about the importance attached to the missing diplomats in England. He reasoned that the Press-relations advisory group in the Kremlin had under-estimated the British interest in the mystery, and the annoyance which the constantly-made, rarely-believed denials had roused in Britain. He felt that they did not realise the first and last questions asked by British reporters, who are as persistent as any in the world, would be "Where are *they*?". The importance of good relations, and all the diplomatic phrases would be lost in this constant barrage, for which B & K would be totally unprepared. It could have led to lost tempers, harsh words—and the failure of their friendship mission.

He thought too that if this point could be put to the Russian leaders simply enough, bluntly enough, rudely enough if necessary, it might make a tiny breach in the silent brick wall.

The trouble was how to get the point in forcefully.

Then, quite suddenly and unexpectedly, Hughes was granted an interview with Mr. Molotov, not then a sick, weary and discredited man, but the powerful Foreign Minister.

In the twenty-four hours before the interview he drafted and redrafted a memorandum "for the eyes of President Bulganin and Mr. Kruschev".

It was not very long, but it was very much to the point. It stated firmly that the two heads of state must realise "that the monstrous nonsense of this 'I-do-not-know' formula would utterly discredit their pending visit to England".

He said that an essential preamble to their visit was the appearance of Burgess and Maclean with some sort of explanation of just what they had done, and why.

The memorandum pointed out that, without this, it was likely that all protestations of friendship would be thought insincere, and that the stories would continue to circulate that the men were dead or in a Russian prison.

Obviously it would not be easy for Kruschev to make an abrupt about-turn and eat his previous words. But it was pointed out that any government which gave sanctuary to aliens would at first respect their wishes to have the matter kept quiet. Of course in succeeding years this has happened more and more frequently with defectors from both sides. Richard Hughes gave his memorandum to the Foreign Secretary in his mirrored, plush, Victorian-style office, then still hung with portraits of a beaming Joseph Stalin.

As a reporter Hughes also pointed out one important thing. While he wanted to see the men and talk to them, he had a deadline. And for the *Sunday Times* that deadline was 5 p.m. on Saturday, February 11, 1956. If Burgess and Maclean were to appear it must be in time for him to get a story for his paper.

On the Saturday, Hughes was waiting. Not too hopefully. It had been a long shot and a lot of other methods had failed to have any effect at all.

In his hotel room, he started packing.

There was nothing by 3 p.m. And nothing by the deadline he had given—5 p.m. He gave up hope.

At 7 p.m. his phone rang and a voice asked him to go to room 101, on the same floor as his own, at 8 p.m.

Just on time he walked along the corridor to room 101. There were three other arrivals. The Reuters man, and correspondents from *Pravda* and the Tass agency.

They knocked and went in.

And there were Burgess and Maclean at last.

They gave no interviews but handed out prepared statements. Then, having proved that they were alive, in good health and spirits, they left.

As Burgess handed a copy of the statement to Richard

Hughes he winked and said without any obvious necessity: "We also want to give this to the *Sunday Times*."

There was only one front-page story the next day, all
over the world.

9

Security?

IF THE Burgess and Maclean story was one of the most important of the century to British newspapers, it was also, perhaps, the greatest disaster in the history of British Intelligence. It exposed unbelievable ineptness, inefficiency and naïvety, and led to the biggest shake-up of M.I.5 and M.I.6 since the outbreak of war. Four senior executives were sacked or resigned, and many others were reprimanded; the victims of this purge today claim bitterly that the real culprits are still in the service. Whether this is true or not, there is no doubt that everyone concerned learned a salutary lesson which was in the end beneficial to all security departments. Four were directly concerned with the investigation: M.I.5, M.I.6, "Q"—the Foreign Office's own internal security office—and the Special Branch.

It is worth describing the work of these departments, as far as it is possible to do so. They are completely separate organisations, though their work is often on parallel lines—a situation that has been commented upon more than once by government enquiries and commissions.

M.I.5 is by far the best known to the public of course, and its name is synonymous with cloak-and-dagger work of every kind. The novels of Ian Fleming and

Dennis Wheatley have created a very sharp and colourful image in the lay mind which for commercial reasons may be entertainingly misleading but which is also, at times, accurate.

M.I.5 is counter-espionage, the tracking down of foreign agents in Britain, while M.I.6 is espionage—the collecting of information from other governments— which is not talked about at all. "Q" section are the "house detectives" of the Foreign Office, and usually amateurs,* posted from other departments to gain two years' experience in the work. The Special Branch is the department that moves in to make the arrests and carry the cases to the courts, when this is possible or desirable.

Between all four there is, or was, a fair degree of squabbling which led to a dangerous lack of liaison, one of the commonest ailments of secret services anywhere. But in Britain, before the Missing Diplomats episode, this lack of liaison reached the proportions of a brick wall

* Commenting on this system, Mr. Harold Macmillan told the Commons on Monday, November 7, 1955: "It has been said that security of the Foreign Office ought to be in the hands of the security service.

"It is true that Foreign Office officials are amateurs in the sense that they do not spend their whole careers upon this job. Nevertheless, they had a corresponding advantage, for this meant that an increasing number of officers in the service, both at home and abroad, gain some experience of security work.

"I am not much attracted by the only other alternative," he went on. "That alternative would be a kind of NKVD or OGPU system in public offices; in other words, that everybody wherever he went or whatever he did, high or low, should be followed by an appropriate officer of a police department."

between the offices concerned. Afterwards, the re-
criminations were furious. M.I.6, whose agents abroad
produced little or nothing in time to stop the flight across
Europe, blamed M.I.5 for letting them get out of
Britain; M.I.5 blamed "Q" for not supplying certain
information quickly enough; and the Special Branch
grumbled that they had been called in too late. The
arguments at the time tended to centre around the
period immediately prior to Departure Day. But the
story begins long before that.

In January 1949, M.I.5 learned that there had been
a leak of information to the Russians of a staggering
nature; information of a kind so secret that only a
handful of people should have had access to it. In practice,
there is no information that only a handful of people
know about—in Whitehall, anyway. For there are many
civil servants, from typists to cipher clerks to radio
operators and personal secretaries and couriers, who
have access to records and documents, even if they are
not in a position to understand them.

Mr. Harold Macmillan, in the House of Commons,
said of this leakage during the debate on the Burgess and
Maclean White Paper: "It is greatly to the credit of the
security authorities that the leakage . . . became known
at all . . . I cannot give the details, but it was an almost
incredible act of skill. . . ."

This fulsome praise was not entirely justified. For
Maclean had been identified as a Communist agent in
1939, and all Britain's security services had done
precisely nothing.

The identification came from a defecting Russian officer, General Krevitsky, who brought with him to the West a vast amount of information about the Soviet secret service and its activities around the world. He was another Petrov, but, like Petrov, he was for some extraordinary reason not taken as seriously as he might have been.

One of the odd facts he produced was that there was in the British Foreign Office an active Soviet agent. He was a young Scotsman, he said, aged about 25, of good family and with excellent connections, who had been an ardent Marxist since University. This young man, Krevitsky went on, lived alone, frequented Bohemian clubs and made friends particularly in artistic and literary circles. Sometimes he wore a cape. The picture was of a Dorian Gray-like character, and complete in almost everything but his name.

Now, this description, it must be admitted, might have fitted a dozen young men in the Foreign Office. But it does not require an incredible act of skill to check on a dozen young men. And if a check HAD been made, the investigators would surely have paused to consider the case of Donald Maclean.

At that time, he was 26. He lived alone in a flat in Chelsea. His friends were, indeed, artists, musicians and writers. He sometimes wore a cape. He could be found every night in the basement and attic clubs of the King's Road and Soho. His Scots name, his excellent connections, his impeccable background—even his known Communist sympathies at University—all these fitted Krevitsky's description, which was still in the file ten years later, in 1949.

Instead of looking in that file, however, M.I.5 spent three years in a futile search that extended from Whitehall to embassies all over the world. When, finally, Maclean was on the short list of suspects, he was followed so unprofessionally that he was aware of it almost from the start, and was able to give them the slip without effort.

Krevitsky's information, incidentally, was sent from the Washington Embassy in 1939 by Lord Lothian—then British Ambassador. He was given the facts by his Counsellor, Sir Victor Mallet, who in turn received it from American intelligence.

Krevitsky was assassinated by Soviet agents in a Washington hotel in 1941.

Now we come to the watch that was put on Maclean when M.I.5 did decide that he was their man. Again, Mr. Macmillan said some strange things about this in the House.

"The decision not to watch him at Tatsfield," he said, "was deliberately taken, after a careful survey had been made of the technical problems involved in keeping him under observation in the neighbourhood of his home. The conclusion was that the risk of putting him on his guard would be too great."

Firstly, the "technical problems" were certainly not beyond the capabilities of M.I.5, who, about the same time and not many miles away, were using an ice-cream van, a garage hand, an empty cottage and a telephone tap on a similar but unconnected problem. Secondly, to speak of "the risk of putting him on his guard" is only laughable. Maclean knew and recognised the men who were tailing him from the start, and with a grim sense of humour nodded to them before they left him at the barrier of Charing Cross station every night.

On one occasion, their taxi even collided with his on his way to the Reform Club. And why, one wonders, was their "incredible skill" not utilised during the final week-end? Could one of the reasons be that it WAS a week-end, or that no one could believe that Maclean would be so un-British as to leave his wife while she was pregnant?

Mr. Macmillan spoke in the debate with the confidence of full knowledge of the steps that had been taken—and the steps that had not been taken. It would be interesting to know when he acquired this knowledge. Certainly Herbert Morrison his predecessor as Foreign Secretary tells a rather different story in his memoirs, in which he writes:

"Personally, I felt that his (Bevin's) intense loathing for disloyalty of any kind, and Communist treachery in particular, would have ensured that he told me of any suspicion even in his remaining weeks of life. In the event, he said nothing, and the disappearance of Burgess and Maclean at the end of May came as a complete surprise to me."

Morrison, though uneasy over the circumstances that

had allowed the two to escape, comes down on the side of M.I. 5 in a later passage:

"I soon satisfied myself that the security forces and the police were doing everything possible to trace the men's movements. With the willing co-operation of the French government, and indeed of all the nations of Western Europe, precise details of their movements as far as the train from Rennes to Paris were soon obtained, contradicting, though nothing could be revealed, most of the bizarre reports appearing in the press."

Which newspapers was the Foreign Secretary reading? While London's morning newspapers were certainly indulging freely in speculation, the popular ones, at least, were certain that the pair were in Moscow, or at least hiding up in some remote part of Europe until arrangements were made for them to cross the Iron Curtain. Were these the "bizarre reports"? Could it not be said that the bland assurances from the Foreign Office, both on and off the record, that the two men had no access to anything really important, were even more bizarre? Or that the most bizarre fact of all was that they actually got away when so many people guessed they were going, and when he himself had signed an interrogation order that was not acted upon?

Many of the men who carried out the investigation have now gone, and the departments have been tightened up to a much greater degree of efficiency, as has been shown publicly by the series of spectacular successes in the last five years. But many of the handicaps remain:

the vast "old boy" network, the niggardly budget (the whole of the secret service, including some new, specialist departments, receives only seven million pounds a year), the tangle of departments, and the simple fact that there are too few people guarding too many secrets (many of which are not worth keeping, anyway), all add up to a heavy burden which is unlikely to be lifted.

One story which illustrates the unreality of life in British counter-espionage work concerns an M.P. who, finding himself forbidden by his doctor to do any kind of work for three months, set himself an exercise in reading. He had just discovered the extent and value of the American Embassy library, a remarkable institution open to the general public, and which is the largest source in Britain of research material about the U.S.

The M.P. decided to write a thesis on the subject of the British aircraft industry, using American magazine files. He had no particular reason for choosing the subject, but as the days went by, he became fascinated by facts and statistics he had never read before. When his report was finished, he was quite proud of it, and several months later took the first opportunity of showing it to an expert.

The expert was a high-ranking Air Force security officer, who said not a word as he read it through to the last full stop. Then he asked in a grave voice: "Can you tell me where you obtained this?"

"I got it from the American Embassy," said the M.P. cheerfully.

"This represents a most serious breach of confidence," said the officer. "If this fell into the wrong hands, it would have disastrous repercussions."

The M.P., at first amused but now alarmed, explained exactly how the report originated. The security man was nonplussed, completely at a loss as to what to say. Finally he asked that the paper should be destroyed or kept in a safe place. "I protested that anyone could have written it," the M.P. told me later, "but he insisted that I should not let anyone see it. In fact, he wanted to take it, but I wouldn't let him. I showed it to my wife, then tore it up. I wondered how many people in security were wasting their time guarding the 'secrets' that could be read about, in detail, in American magazines."

The conservative attitude of M.I. 5 and 6, and "Q", must cause considerable amusement to their counterparts abroad. Which other country would allow one of its agents to be hauled up in court on a driving charge, his name and address revealed and publicity assured by having the prosecution say: "It would not be in the public interest to disclose this man's occupation"? The man in this particular case was accused—and acquitted—of being drunk in charge of a car. The car contained top-secret documents, and in the man's pockets was found a tiny tape-recorder with a wrist-watch microphone. All this was aired in a country court-room, and no doubt made interesting reading for any foreign agent who studied the newspapers. Was it really necessary in the interests of justice to talk about tape-recorders and top-secret documents, and arouse curiosity about the man's occupation? After all, when a famous homosexual actor was accused of importuning, he was described on the charge-sheet as a clerk. . . .

Another weird illustration of the strange doings of Intelligence comes from two men who were on holiday in Switzerland in the first week of June 1951. George Bauens had just finished a six-months' job as steward on the *Queen Mary*. With a friend he decided to tour Switzerland on a motor-scooter, and eventually arrived at a little-known mountain resort where he had once worked as a waiter.

Sitting in the glass-fronted terrace lounge of an hotel there, they spotted far below them, a rucksacked figure toiling up the twisty, rough and stony track. After half an hour a perspiring, bearded gentleman, seemingly in the last stages of exhaustion, tapped on the window, making signs with an open mouth indicating hunger or thirst or both. It transpired that he was an Englishman who had run out of money and had not eaten for two days. They asked him to join them, ordered a meal and asked how they could help. But their guest was much more interested in them than in giving information about himself. It was not until an hour had gone by that the stranger ruefully admitted that his story was untrue. "I am a British security man," he said. "I heard a report that you were in the vicinity, and that you might be Burgess and Maclean."

There were hundreds of other false reports, of course, from all over Europe, and many genuine clues were turned up, too. But on balance, it appears that most of the concrete tips given to M.I.5 arrived *before* the men vanished.

One of the oddest pieces of information received by the department came from a village chemist in Westerham, Kent.

Mr. Ernest White had become more than a little troubled by the strange activities of one of his customers. Mr. White, like so many chemists, undertook the developing and printing of film and snapshots. Most of them were so routine that he did not even look at them as he packed them into the little yellow Kodak envelopes. But one man brought in film that was different. So different, in fact, that he would not allow Mr. White to handle it. One Saturday morning, when the man first appeared in the busy little shop, he asked if he could develop it himself . . . just a few rolls, he said apologetically, but the exposures were rather tricky and he would feel happier if he could do it himself. He hired the darkroom at the back of the shop for an hour, developed his film, paid and left.

But he returned with the same request . . . more and more frequently. He tidied up after himself meticulously and, in fact, was no trouble at all, but Mr. White found one evening a screwed-up, damp print, rejected as over-developed. It was almost black, but the few words that were visible agitated Mr. White very much indeed. For the picture was of a document, and from casual conversation the chemist knew that his customer was a Foreign Office employee. Putting all he knew together and adding a dash of suspicion, he called in the police, who informed M.I. 5.

Unfortunately for Whitehall, the tip-off was a little late—or at any rate, there was not enough time for M.I. 5 to check the story thoroughly, they said. Which was a pity. Because the customer was Donald Maclean. . . .

Who are the men who work for M.I. 5, 6 and the other secret services? What are they like?

There are very few James Bonds. The true picture of a security officer, or one that might be typical, is of a man in his forties, a service or ex-service officer above the rank of captain, tough but probably on the tubby side, with a record of painstaking promotion in a department such as the cipher or personnel office.

He will be married, with a stable domestic life and the background of a sound education in which he might have specialised in modern languages or philosophy. His knowledge of several para-military subjects such as ballistics or communications will certainly be above average, but first and foremost he is required to have a knowledge of people. In fact, his qualifications will be similar to those of the manager of a city bank who has seen a long period of war service.

The jobs to which they are assigned include such mundane tasks as checking hundreds of pages of transcripts of tapped telephone conversations or reading endless ship and aircraft passenger lists, searching for perhaps one name in ten thousand. Screening prospective employees in government departments is a large and monotonous part of their work; at one time it was claimed that M.I.5 were clearing 5,000 a week.

They can be called upon to double as Queen's Messengers, carrying diplomatic bags anywhere in the world, or they can be set to watching a Bloomsbury flat for weeks on end from the discomfort of an attic window opposite. They can be disguised as railway porters, chauffeurs, insurance salesmen, journalists or company directors; M.I.6 men stationed abroad are usually on the payroll of huge international organisations such as oil or insurance companies.

The men who go to the active trouble spots are generally Special Branch officers such as John Prendergast, who has used his brains and his revolver in such places as Cyprus, Hong Kong, Palestine and Kenya— where he was awarded the George Medal for bravery.

Salaries of the top men go up to £4,000, but the head of a section is unlikely to get more than half that, and "expenses" are scrutinised very carefully indeed. So there is little glamour and no money by industrial standards in the work. The men in the field are dedicated to doing a job conscientiously and for its own sake, but there is no doubt that at the time of the Burgess and Maclean affair, there were many people whose inadequacies were being cloaked by inactivity.

In all the official comments on the blunders of the secret service, there is the overriding argument that no one wants to give too much power to M.I.5; no one, in fact, wants a police state in Britain. No one does, surely. But the opinion of people who have far more than the layman's knowledge of M.I.5 is that in the 1950s, anyway, the men responsible for screening others should have been screened more carefully themselves. As Burgess has said in Moscow of one M.I.5 man he knew: "I'm glad he didn't get fired. He didn't mean any harm—and I don't know what other job he could do!"

Herbert Morrison has something to say about the security services and the Missing Diplomats' case in his book.

"The continued employment of Maclean and Burgess," he writes, "in view of their lapses, and the failure to check on their communist sympathies while they were Cambridge undergraduates, was a reflection on the Foreign Office.

"In fairness, it must be pointed out that men of their generation, going to university in the early thirties at the zenith of the world depression, were very prone to have communist leanings and to regard the Soviet Union as a paradise in a world to which capitalism had brought disaster. Unquestioning observance of some rule about dismissal for all those who had ever suffered the growing pains of flirting with communism could only have produced a British version of the McCarthy investigations in the U.S.A., hardly a desirable situation. Still, added to their back record of personal conduct, their communist record was not irrevelant.

"Nevertheless, I felt that the whole security system of the Foreign Office needed to be revised, and in July 1951 I set up a committee of enquiry to consider the security checks on Foreign Office staff, to examine the regulations and practices as regards security and to report on any desirable changes. In November the committee reported its recommendations for a more extensive security check on Foreign Service officers, and this now applies.

"In a world where the ruthless efficiency of the Soviet espionage system never relaxes, it would be unwise to affirm that another Maclean-Burgess affair can never occur, but so far as it is humanly possible, given the need to maintain the British concept of individual freedom of thought, the case should remain a unique one."

10

At Home in Exile

TODAY, BURGESS and Maclean are not happy men, by any means. But it must not be assumed that they are prisoners, either. Since their arrival in Russia their careers have diverged just as they would have done in the West.

Burgess says that when they reached the Soviet Union after their dramatic flight there was no red carpet treatment. The Russians were courteous, polite hosts, interested in everything they had to say and anxious for their comfort. Underneath, though, there must have been a tinge of suspicion, a feeling of reserve, towards them. In spite of their background of service to communism, were they in fact "planted" by the wily British secret service? Only time would convince them that they were not.

In those first months the two runaways were kept out of Moscow, well concealed by the anonymity of a small industrial town. They shared a worker's apartment, and this was rather like being moved from Old Bond Street to a council flat in Crewe. In their four rooms they wrote their first reports for the NVD, the Foreign Ministry and for anyone else who cared to call, and from these the Soviets made their first evaluation of them.

The secrets they poured out so willingly no doubt cost

the West lives and prestige and money, and certainly one of the far-reaching consequences was a reorganisation of the British security system, no less than the reorganisation which followed, more recently, the Blake case. It would be interesting to know which of the two men was regarded more highly by the Russians then; in Britain, there were divided opinions. "Burgess," Herbert Morrison wrote in his book, "was the more lively and potentially dangerous partner. I did not meet him, so far as I can recall. I gathered that he was an intelligent and rather bumptious young man—a typical career diplomat. As personal assistant to the Minister of State, Hector McNeil, he had access to the most secret documents. McNeil liked him, regarded him as a live wire, with a pleasant manner and considerable intelligence; indeed, he had pressed for Burgess as his personal assistant.

"It is strange, therefore, that the security authorities regarded Maclean as the principal suspect. He had far less opportunity to read secret documents and was, as a result of his Cairo breakdown, less highly regarded."

One can only assume from this that Morrison did not know of Maclean's presence at the Chicago atom conference, and that he did not know, either, that Maclean was looked upon as the Foreign Office expert on atomic energy. As such, he had access to the secrets not only of Britain, but of her allies too—or such secrets as Britain was trusted with, following the defections of Nunn May, Fuchs and Pontecorvo.

Those who doubt his standing in this sphere may be interested in this story, hitherto unknown.

Raymond Blackburn, M.P. for Northfields (Birmingham) in 1950, was the Labour Party's Parliamentary expert on atomic energy. He had studied the subject intensively and was Chairman of the Parliamentary Commission on Atomic Energy. Sir Winston Churchill had said of him: "He is the keeper of Britain's conscience on the atom."

Just before the commencement of a series of disarmament talks in Geneva, Blackburn was due to take the Adjournment on Atomic Energy. M.P.s wanted to know what Britain's contribution would be, what thoughts we had had, what suggestions we were to make; in other words, where we stood on nuclear disarmament.

While he was wrestling with the outline of the speech, the telephone rang in his office. It was Christopher Mayhew, Parliamentary Under Secretary of State for Foreign Affairs. He would like to show round, he said, a Foreign Office man with great experience of the subject; not a scientist, but a diplomat who had closely followed recent developments in the nuclear fields of West and East, and who was regarded by the Foreign Office as their "expert on the subject".

An hour later the expert arrived in Blackburn's office. His name: Donald Maclean. "I treated him with the respect I thought he deserved," says Blackburn today. "He really did know a lot about the subject and I did not in the least mind Mayhew sending him along.

However, it became apparent when we really got down to business that in several important ideas and points of policy we were completely at variance. We argued for hours. I remember saying that the Russians had not agreed to aerial inspection, but he insisted that they had. I said that they most certainly had not, but, again, he repeated that they had; not in public, but privately, yes.

"I felt that Maclean obviously knew a great deal about the background of international agreement (or disagreement) on the atom. I amended one or two points, although I cannot say that any of my revisions were on main points.

"Incidentally, there was a curious sequel. A few days after I had spoken in the House, Mr. Vishinsky, then Soviet Foreign Minister, took the unusual step of quoting parts of it at the United Nations, praising its 'fair-mindedness', its 'objectivity' and so on. By coincidence, the parts he chose were specifically Maclean's."

This is some indication of the way Maclean worked. This one incident alone makes nonsense of the claim that he knew little about our atom secrets. It makes sense of Acheson's spontaneous: "My God, he knew everything!" remark.

So, if Morrison is correct, and Burgess was more valuable to the Soviets than Maclean, then their defection was indeed a national disaster.

Both men, anyway, no doubt regaled their hosts with scores of stories of this kind; they must have enjoyed an attentive, and often amused, audience. They became advisers to the Foreign Ministry—though not with desks and telephones and secretaries, as in the Foreign Office. Western collaborators in Moscow are more often dealt with on the "old boy" net: little dinner parties, week-ends in a country dacha, purposeful gentlemen who "drop in" for a chat, and requests for articles for specialist magazines.

When the time came for them to appear on the social scene in Moscow, both were given a middle-class professional front which, if not advertisement to entice potential defectors, was comfortable enough. Each had cars (chauffeur-driven, at first), each had pleasant apartments furnished in the heavy Victorian fashion that spells success in the capital, and both, seemingly, had plenty of money—though there was little to spend it on that could have been to their taste.

Their direct employers were offshoots of the State Publishing House, an organisation of vast complexity and power, controlling the reading habits of the Soviet public and giving shelter to a surprisingly large number of Westerners. It is an all-embracing body; whether you are seventeen or seventy, whether you were an ambassador or a bank clerk, leader-writer or typewriter mechanic, if you speak only English or Hindustani, there is, inevitably, a job for you in the Publishing House. Nobody knows how many thousand employees it had, directly and indirectly, but its roof covers a great multitude of Western political sinners, anyway.

Whether Burgess and Maclean found this huge machine an easy place to work in is doubtful. Its policies must certainly have taken a little getting used to. A Russian friend who is a colleague of Maclean told me that a few months ago he had been commissioned to write a book on the foreign policy of a Western country in which he had lived (as a member of the Soviet Embassy staff) for seven years.

He had to produce this book at great speed as it was required urgently, and so worked late into the night, every night. His typing was not of a professional standard, so he had to hire a stenographer at his own expense, and as the manuscript was more than 100,000 words, this was considerable. He finished on time, delivered the book to his chiefs and waited for the money. Instead, he received a polite note saying that though his work was of great interest, it was not as good as "the other one". He quickly discovered that this referred to another manuscript on the same subject that had been commissioned from another author at the same time!

This, it was explained to him, was a new system, copied from the West—"and if that," the Russian told me, darkly, "is your capitalist competition, you can keep it!"

It can be assumed that neither Burgess nor Maclean were responsible for that idea! What they claim that they have been instrumental in doing is to introduce a more catholic approach to Western literature, and it seems likely that this occupies a great deal of their time, as their diplomatic advisory value, after all these out-of-touch years, is practically zero.

Maclean (using the name of Frazer) continues to be the conscientious bureaucrat that he was in the West, and the transition from West to East, with all the harrowing experiences of the two journeys, seems to have stabilised the marriage (the only contrary report being that Melinda recently threatened to leave her husband for a Russian major). Like her husband, Melinda is still an ardent Communist, but those who have met them in Moscow and in Britain say that they can sense a deep-down dissatisfaction. This may, of course, spring from a yearning for some of the old material comforts and surroundings they once enjoyed; in Moscow, a spade is a spade, and never mind what it looks like. Beauty is in the Bolshoi.

Melinda's dresses and her husband's shirts come from Copenhagen and Helsinki in small quantities; they have an allowance of foreign currency which enables them to buy a few luxuries by mail-order, but not on the scale of Western correspondents or diplomats, who, if the Macleans were not so completely unapproachable, would be delighted to help out with domestic items. The death of Lady Maclean may alter their standard of living, of course, as the British government has consented to the transfer of funds to Moscow, treating both Maclean and Burgess as emigrants. A legacy of several thousand pounds in sterling has presumably gone through the normal channels.

Burgess is by no means so financially secure, or so proud, but then his is a different story. When he talked with Tom Driberg seven years ago he was a man still buoyant and exhilarated by the heady air of intellectual Moscow; today he is sinking into the same mire of vice and self-indulgence that would have been his future in London. He has outraged guests at diplomatic parties in the same way that he did in New York; only now there is no excuse for him, there are no targets for his insults— or no targets that he could prudently insult. His behaviour is more keenly watched than in the old days, too. His face has been seen at fewer and fewer cosmopolitan parties, as he is dropped from more and more official invitation lists.

His Volga car has been taken away (after, it is rumoured, two traffic offences similar to those in Virginia) and he has been moved from one apartment to another, until now he lives in one room. As he slipped lower and lower down the social ladder, Burgess began to let himself go sexually. Invoking the creed of to each according to his needs, he took Tolya, a peasant youth who plays the accordion, as his companion.

How this was fixed with the Soviet authorities, and to which Ministry he had to go to obtain permission for this arrangement, has been the subject of ribald speculation. But, as usual, Burgess could not remain faithful, and slipped away as often as he could to the Black Sea coast, the Soviet Riviera, where one night the inevitable happened, and he spent the night in a police cell after attempting to importune sailors.

In Moscow, among Westerners, he is pitied. He still retains his old charm and wit and easy conversation, but there is no substance any more behind the amusing, know-all front. He wanders from flat to flat, from meal to meal, from drink to drink, with a badly-concealed aimlessness, discussing the rights of Russia and the wrongs of America and deploring the fact that most of the Russian-Jewish tailors left during the revolution.

He talks about his mother (now too old to visit him, as she once did) and about politics. Perhaps the Englishman most in his confidence is Jeremy Wolfenden, another Old Etonian, correspondent for the *Daily Telegraph* and son of Sir John. But his conversational favours are so freely distributed—unlike Maclean's—that it is no longer interesting to say: "I met Guy Burgess."

There are very few people indeed who can claim that of Donald Maclean. One of his closest friends is an Australian author and journalist, Wilfred Burchett, who is the most remarkable of all the voluntary residents of Moscow. An ex-*Daily Express* war correspondent, he changed ideological sides after Hiroshima (his description of the city after the Bomb was the first out of Japan, and had tremendous political repercussions) and has since integrated himself into Soviet life completely, while retaining all his old Western friendships—a position which Maclean must envy. And while Burchett has no hesitation in saying what he thinks to anyone, regardless of official approval or not, Maclean has developed a rubber-stamp attitude of agreement with whatever is current policy.

A friend who knew him well in London once met

the Macleans in Leningrad. They were staying in the same hotel on a short leave; Donald was showing Melinda the city for the first time. The three spent a week-end sightseeing and remembering old times and old places. "He was just like his old self," the friend told me, "but I got the impression that he would have said a lot more if Melinda hadn't been there. She is really the fiery one, you know—everything that is Russian is marvellous, everything that isn't, isn't. Donald is not like that at all, though on some subjects he is getting on that way. I was terribly glad to see them both again, but I found their attitudes rather depressing in their conformity. Donald was an individualist. Now he isn't, any more."

Postscript

OF THE many unsolved mysteries of the Burgess and Maclean story, the latest is in some ways the most puzzling. Why on that morning in April 1962 were the warrants for the arrests of the two issued? Whence arose the rumour that they were on their way home? These questions have never been answered.

One not at all unlikely theory is that a visitor to Moscow from Britain met Burgess casually and was asked by him: "What do you think I shall get if I come back and stand trial? Do you think I'll be tried at all?" For these are the questions that Burgess asks everyone he meets from home. They are academic, arising only from his natural curiosity. Those who know him treat them as no more interesting than questions about the weather.

If, however, an impressionable visitor was to hear those questions from Burgess for the first time he might have been excited enough to pass on the answers to M.I.5, maybe with a little embroidery in the telling. This could have forced a decision to frighten them—or, rather, Burgess—away, by staging a drama involving the full majesty of the law, under the arc lights of the press and television. I say Burgess, as distinct from Maclean, since I am convinced that no one in M.I.5,

M.I.6 or "Q" or the Special Branch was *ever* told that Maclean was returning, or was likely to. He is dedicated to his ideology; Burgess is a little tired of the conformity that goes with it. He is still restless, dissatisfied, adventurous—and rather hurt that so many should think badly of him.

As he once said: "How else, at this moment of history, can one behave, except badly?"